The Savings Rate Playbook

How Much to Actually Save at Every Income Level, and Why the "Save 20%" Rule Is Wrong for Almost Everyone

Daniel Cross

First edition, 2026

Published by Daniel Cross

Contents

Foreword

A few years into advising people on their money, I started keeping a private tally of a specific kind of conversation. Someone would tell me, almost apologetically, that they weren't saving 20% of their income — the number they'd absorbed from a podcast, a coworker, a parent who'd said it so many times it calcified into gospel. Then we'd sit down with their actual numbers, and it became obvious within minutes that 20% was mathematically impossible for them without going hungry or living somewhere unsafe. The guilt they carried wasn't a personal failing. It was the residue of a rule never built for their income in the first place.

The tally kept growing, but not in the direction I expected. About as often as I met someone crushed by a target they couldn't hit, I met someone who'd hit it easily, felt good about clearing the bar, and had no idea they were leaving enormous compounding on the table — the same flat number that broke the first person quietly undersold the second. Two people, same rule, opposite failure. Not a rule with a few edge cases. Wrong about the actual math for most people using it.

Both needed someone to do the arithmetic that "save 20%" was always supposed to be a shorthand for, and never actually is. Fixed costs don't scale with income the way percentages assume. A rate cruel at one income is lazy at another. Debt changes the math. A new baby changes it, temporarily. Starting at 45 instead of 25 changes it in a way no flat percentage was built to account for.

This book is that arithmetic, chapter by chapter, with real numbers worked through. It doesn't argue that saving matters — you already know that, or you wouldn't have picked this up. It argues that the specific number matters more than the fact of saving something, and that the number is calculable, not inherited from whichever advice column reached you first. My own stake is simple: I've watched the wrong number cause real harm in both directions, toward people who blamed themselves for math that was never going to work, and toward people who never found out how much better their own math could have been. I'd like this to be the last time either mistake gets made on a borrowed rule instead of a real one.

— Daniel Cross

Introduction

Ask ten different sources what percentage of income you should save, and you'll get some version of the same answer: 20%, sometimes 15%, occasionally 10% as a floor. It's repeated so often, across so many books, apps, and casual conversations, that it's stopped sounding like a claim that could be checked and started sounding like a fact of nature — as fixed and universal as the boiling point of water. It isn't. It's a single number applied to every income, every household size, every stage of life, every level of existing debt, as if none of those things changed what "correct" actually means.

This book exists because that flat number breaks in two directions at once, and almost nobody talks about the second one. At the bottom of the income range, 20% is often not a stretch goal — it's arithmetic that doesn't close. Rent, food, insurance, transportation, and basic utilities have a real dollar floor that doesn't shrink just because a paycheck is smaller, and for a large number of households, that floor consumes more than 80% of take-home pay before a single discretionary dollar is spent. Telling that household to save 20% isn't ambitious advice. It's advice that can only be followed by cutting into things that shouldn't be cut — food quality, medical care, a safe place to live — which isn't saving. It's damage with a savings label on it.

At the top of the income range, the same flat number fails in the opposite direction, and this failure is quieter because it doesn't look like a crisis. A household earning well above their fixed-cost floor who saves a flat 20% is often leaving a huge amount of sustainable additional savings on the table, because 20% of a number with enormous headroom above it is a much smaller fraction of *available* room than 20% of a number with almost no headroom at all. Nobody notices this failure the way they notice the first one, because nothing goes wrong in the moment — the bills get paid, the vacation happens, the savings account grows steadily. It's only decades later, at a retirement number that's smaller than it could have been for the exact same lifestyle, that the cost of an artificially low ceiling becomes visible, and by then it's too late to recover the compounding that a slightly higher rate, sustained for slightly longer, would have produced.

Both failures come from the same root cause: a percentage of *gross or take-home income* is the wrong denominator. What should actually determine your savings rate isn't your income alone — it's your income relative to your true fixed-cost floor, adjusted for whatever debt, life stage, and goals are really sitting on your specific balance sheet right now. Two people earning the identical salary can have wildly different correct savings rates, because one has three years of a car loan and a toddler in daycare and the other has neither. A single flat percentage can't see any of that. The math in this book can.

This book doesn't cover how to automate a savings rate once you've determined it — building the account structure, the automatic transfers, the triggers that move money without relying on willpower. That's genuinely useful and worth its own book, and a companion book in this library, *The Automatic Wealth System*, covers exactly that mechanical territory in full. This book stops one step earlier, at the question that has to be answered first and rarely gets asked directly: given your specific income, your specific fixed costs, your specific debt, your specific life stage, and your specific goals, what rate should actually be automated? Getting the mechanics right on the wrong number just automates the wrong outcome faster and more reliably. This book is about getting the number right before it ever touches an automatic transfer.

Here's what's ahead. The first chapter builds the core diagnostic — the fixed-cost floor test — that explains precisely why a flat percentage breaks and gives you a replacement framework built on your actual numbers instead of a borrowed average. From there, the book walks through real math by income bracket, showing what a sustainable rate looks like at several different points on the income spectrum, worked all the way through with real dollar figures. Later chapters handle the situations a flat rule can't touch at all: adjusting your rate around high-interest debt, resetting it temporarily through a major life transition, running the catch-up math if you're starting later than you'd like, calculating a rate against income that doesn't arrive in tidy, predictable amounts, and deciding how to split whatever you're saving between tax-advantaged retirement accounts and money you can actually reach. The book closes with a chapter most savings advice never gets to at all — the ceiling. There's a

real point past which more saving stops producing more benefit, and knowing where that point sits for your own situation is as much a part of getting the number right as knowing your floor.

A word on how to read this book. Each chapter follows the same shape: a real situation you'll likely recognize, the actual mechanics of why the standard advice fails there, a concrete framework with the arithmetic laid out, and a worked example carrying real numbers through the entire calculation. Dollar figures throughout are illustrative — chosen to make the math concrete and easy to follow, not to represent a benchmark you should copy directly into your own plan. Substitute your own numbers into every formula in this book; that substitution is the actual product it's trying to hand you, not the specific figures used to demonstrate it.

A word on what this book won't do. It won't tell you which bank or brokerage to use, or how to build the account structure that holds your savings once the rate is set — that's mechanical territory this book deliberately leaves to its companion volume. It won't diagnose why saving feels emotionally hard, why a specific number triggers anxiety, or what wired-in reflex might be driving an urge to spend instead of save — that's real territory, and it belongs to a different kind of book entirely, one built around psychology rather than arithmetic. What this book will do is teach you the actual math well enough that you can calculate your own correct rate, defend it with real numbers when a flat rule tells you it's too low or unnecessarily high, and adjust it correctly as your income, debt, and life stage change — which they will, more than once, over a working life.

A word on the specific numbers used throughout this book. Every dollar figure, interest rate, and assumed return in every worked example is a real, plausible number chosen to make a particular calculation concrete, not a data point pulled from any specific published survey or lookup table for a specific year. Where this book cites an actual published benchmark, framework, or piece of research — an age-based savings milestone, a widely used replacement-ratio study, a specific researcher's work on sustainable withdrawal rates — it says so explicitly and points you to the real source in the Notes & Further Reading section at the back, rather than presenting a borrowed figure as though it were the book's own original math.

The two categories, illustrative arithmetic and cited external research, are kept deliberately distinct throughout, so you always know which kind of number you're looking at.

A final word on who this book is for. It's for the household earning near the bottom of a local income range who has spent years feeling like a personal failure for never hitting a savings percentage that, once the real math is run, turns out to have been mathematically impossible for their specific floor in the first place. It's equally for the household earning comfortably above their floor who has been quietly and unknowingly leaving substantial money uncollected because nobody ever showed them a framework that scales past a flat percentage's ceiling. It's for the late starter doing the arithmetic for the first time and needing an honest, calculable path forward instead of either false comfort or unearned panic. And it's for anyone, at any income, who has simply never been shown that a savings rate is something to calculate rather than something to inherit. If any of these describes you, the chapters ahead are built to work from your specific numbers, not a generic average of everyone's.

By the end, you won't have a percentage handed to you from an average you've never seen the inputs of. You'll have a method for calculating your own, and the confidence that comes from knowing exactly why it's correct for your situation specifically, not despite it.

Let's do the math.

Chapter 1 — Why "Save 20%" Breaks

The situation

Two households sit down, in the same week, to figure out whether they're saving enough. The first earns $34,000 a year after tax, working full-time in a role that doesn't offer much room for negotiation on pay in the near term. Rent, groceries at a realistic level, a used car payment, insurance, and utilities add up to roughly $2,650 of their $2,833 monthly take-home pay. They've heard the 20% rule from a podcast their sister recommended, and they've been quietly beating themselves up for months over never getting close to it. The math, done honestly, shows why: 20% of their income is $566 a month, and after their true fixed costs, they have $183 left over for everything else — food beyond the grocery baseline, clothing, anything unexpected, and whatever savings survives the month. The 20% target isn't a stretch. It's a number larger than their entire discretionary budget combined.

The second household earns $310,000 a year after tax, roughly $25,800 a month. Their fixed costs — a mortgage well within their means, insurance, utilities, groceries, two car payments — run about $8,200 a month. They've also heard the 20% rule, and they're hitting it comfortably: $5,160 a month moves automatically into savings and investments, and they feel, reasonably, like responsible savers. What they haven't calculated is that after fixed costs, they have $17,600 a month of room before touching a single dollar earmarked for savings — and their 20% target is consuming less than a third of that room. They're not failing by any visible measure. They're just leaving a very large amount of sustainable, comfortable additional savings sitting in a lifestyle that's already fully funded, without ever running the number that would show them exactly how much.

Neither household is doing anything wrong in the sense of poor judgment. Both are following the same widely repeated advice. The advice itself is the problem, and it's worth being precise about why, because the fix isn't "try harder" for the first household or "feel guiltier" for the second. It's a different calculation entirely.

The mechanics

A percentage-of-income savings rule implicitly assumes that fixed costs scale proportionally with income — that someone earning three times as much has fixed costs three times as large, so that a flat percentage lands at roughly the same *relative* difficulty for everyone. This assumption is false, and it's false in a specific, measurable way. Fixed costs have a real dollar floor set by the actual price of housing, food, insurance, and transportation in a given area — a floor that moves far more slowly than income does, and that doesn't scale down proportionally just because someone earns less, or scale up proportionally just because someone earns more.

Consider what this means in practice. A basic, realistic monthly floor for one person in a moderate-cost area — modest rent, groceries, a functioning car or transit pass, health insurance, utilities — might run somewhere in the neighborhood of $2,000 to $2,600 depending on location, whether someone earns $30,000 a year or $300,000 a year. That floor doesn't triple for the person earning ten times as much, because there's a limit to how much housing, food, and insurance genuinely cost before the additional spending becomes lifestyle inflation rather than a fixed necessity. What changes with income isn't the floor — it's the size of the gap between the floor and take-home pay. A person earning near the floor has almost no gap. A person earning well above it has an enormous one.

This is the entire reason a flat percentage produces two opposite failures. Applied against income with almost no gap above the floor, a flat percentage asks for money that doesn't exist without cutting into the floor itself — which means cutting into rent, food, or insurance, not into anything genuinely discretionary. Applied against income with a large gap above the floor, a flat percentage captures only a modest slice of that gap, leaving a much larger amount of truly sustainable savings unclaimed simply because the rule was never built to look at the gap in the first place — only at the income.

There's a related mechanism that explains why the second household's failure is so much harder to notice than the first's. A savings rate calculated against gross or take-home income treats every dollar of income as equally "saveable," when in reality every dollar below the fixed-cost floor is genuinely unavailable — it's already spoken for — and every dollar above the floor is, in a real sense, more available for saving than the dollars below it, because spending it isn't covering something you can't live without. A rate that ignores this distinction treats a dollar earned by someone at the floor identically to a dollar earned by someone well above it, when the two dollars are doing completely different jobs in each household's actual budget.

The framework: the fixed-cost floor test

The fix is to stop calculating a savings rate against income and start calculating it against the gap between income and your true fixed-cost floor. This is a three-step test, and it replaces the flat-percentage approach entirely.

Step 1 — Calculate your true fixed-cost floor, not your current spending. This is not the same as your current budget. It's the minimum you'd need to cover housing, food at a realistic (not bare-bones, not inflated) level, insurance, transportation, minimum debt payments, and utilities, if you had to strip out every discretionary dollar this month. Be honest in both directions — don't inflate the floor by including a streaming subscription or a gym membership dressed up as "essential," and don't deflate it by pricing groceries or insurance at an unrealistic minimum you couldn't actually sustain. The floor is a real number, not an aspirational one and not a punitive one.

Step 2 — Calculate your gap: take-home income minus the floor. This is the pool of money that's genuinely available to be split between savings and discretionary spending. It is, for most people, a meaningfully smaller number than their total income, and for people near the floor, it can be a startlingly small number — which is itself useful information, not a discouraging one, because it tells you honestly what's actually possible right now rather than what a borrowed percentage assumes is possible.

Step 3 — Set your savings rate as a percentage of the gap, not a percentage of income, and let that percentage rise as the gap widens. A gap that's small relative to income supports a smaller percentage of itself going to savings, because discretionary spending still needs some room to exist — nobody sustains a plan with zero flexibility for long. A gap that's large relative to income supports a much larger percentage of itself going to savings, because there's more room above the floor to work with before discretionary spending starts feeling constrained. Chapter 2 builds out the specific math for what "smaller" and "larger" percentages actually look like at different points on this spectrum — this chapter is about establishing the test itself, which is the same test at every income level even though the resulting number differs enormously.

This reframing does something a flat percentage can't: it produces a number that's honest about what's actually available, instead of a number borrowed from an average household's average expenses that may bear no resemblance to yours. It also explains, mechanically, why the same 20% figure can feel impossible to one household and effortless to another — they're not experiencing the same rule differently because of different discipline. They're being asked completely different things by the same number, because the number was never built to account for the floor in the first place.

Worked example

Return to the two households from the opening. The first earns $2,833 a month take-home with a genuine fixed-cost floor of $2,650. Their gap is $183. Twenty percent of their income asked for $566 — more than three times their entire available gap. Using the fixed-cost floor test instead, a sustainable starting rate against a gap this thin is modest: something in the range of 15 to 25% of the gap itself, not the income, which for this household is roughly $27 to $46 a month. That number will sound discouragingly small compared to the 20%-of-income figure they'd internalized, and it's worth being direct about why it's still the right number: it's a number that can actually be sustained every month without eating into rent or groceries, which makes it real savings instead of an intention that quietly cannibalizes the floor three months in. As their income grows — a raise, a second income stream, a lower-cost living situation — the gap widens, and the sustainable percentage of that gap rises with it, covered fully in Chapter 2.

The second household earns $25,800 a month with a fixed-cost floor of $8,200, leaving a gap of $17,600. Their current rate of $5,160 a month is 20% of income, but it's only about 29% of their actual available gap. Using the floor test, a household with this much room above their fixed costs can sustainably direct a much larger share of the gap to savings — commonly somewhere in the 45 to 60% range, depending on their specific goals and risk tolerance, which for this household would mean somewhere between roughly $7,900 and $10,600 a month, not $5,160. That's a difference of $2,700 to $5,400 a month, or roughly $32,000 to $65,000 a year, sitting unclaimed simply because a flat percentage never asked the household to look at their actual gap. Compounded over even a decade, that gap in contributions is the difference between a comfortable retirement and a genuinely early one, or between funding a single goal and funding two.

Why the flat rule persists anyway

It's worth understanding why "save 20%" keeps circulating despite breaking this badly at both ends of the income range, because the reason isn't dishonesty — it's simplicity winning out over accuracy in a context where accuracy takes real effort to communicate. A single, memorable number is easy to repeat, easy to put in a headline, and easy to feel good or bad about without doing any actual arithmetic. The fixed-cost floor test in this chapter takes longer to explain and requires you to actually calculate your own floor, which is real work most casual financial advice isn't built to ask of its audience. That tradeoff — a memorable but wrong number versus an accurate but effortful one — explains most of why flat percentage rules dominate popular financial advice even though anyone who does the arithmetic on a real budget can see where they break.

This doesn't mean flat benchmarks are worthless as a rough anchor for comparison — a well-researched age-based or income-based benchmark can be a useful sanity check, and later chapters in this book reference several real ones. What it means is that a benchmark should be treated as a starting comparison point, not a target to force onto a budget that can't sustain it, or a ceiling that stops a budget with real room from doing better. The distinction between "benchmark to compare against" and "number to force compliance with" is the entire difference between useful and harmful in how these rules typically get used.

A second worked example: the same income, two different floors

Flat percentage rules also miss something the fixed-cost floor test catches naturally: two households earning the identical income can have completely different correct savings rates because their floors differ, not their incomes. Consider two individuals, each earning $4,600 a month take-home, living in different regions. The first lives in a high-cost metro area where a modest one-bedroom apartment alone runs $2,400 a month; their total fixed-cost floor, including insurance, groceries, and transportation, comes to $3,650, leaving a gap of $950. The second lives in a lower-cost region where a comparable modest apartment runs $1,100 a month; their total floor comes to $2,300, leaving a gap of $2,300 — more than double the first person's, on the identical income.

A flat percentage rule would ask both of these people to save the same amount, because it only ever looks at the income line, never the floor beneath it. The fixed-cost floor test correctly identifies that the second person has genuinely more room to save sustainably, not because they're more disciplined or make better choices, but because their actual cost of living leaves more of their income available. This isn't a claim that geography is destiny — the first person may have other reasons for living where they live, including career opportunities that eventually raise their income well past the second person's. It's simply a demonstration that income alone, the only input a flat percentage rule ever looks at, is not sufficient information to calculate a correct savings rate. The floor is not optional information. It's the other half of the equation a flat rule quietly ignores.

Common objections and how to handle them

"Isn't a low floor-based rate for someone near the fixed-cost line just an excuse to save too little?" No — it's an honest number instead of a false one. A household following the fixed-cost floor test and calculating a small sustainable rate isn't choosing to save less than they should; they're discovering the truth about what's currently possible, which is more useful than chasing an impossible target that either fails every month or gets hit by cutting into rent or food. The floor test doesn't cap what a household can eventually save — it tells them honestly where they stand right now, and Chapter 2 covers exactly how that number should rise as income grows or the floor shrinks.

"Doesn't a higher rate for a household well above the floor just mean sacrificing quality of life unnecessarily?" This is worth taking seriously rather than dismissing, and Chapter 8 addresses it directly and at length — there's a genuine ceiling past which more saving stops producing more benefit, and this book doesn't argue for maximizing a savings rate without limit. What this chapter argues is narrower: a household with a large gap above their floor should be making a deliberate, informed choice about how much of that gap to save, rather than defaulting to a number that happens to match a flat rule built for households in a completely different position. An informed 45% might be exactly the wrong number for a specific household's goals — but so might an uninformed 20% that was never actually calculated against their real gap in the first place.

"What if I can't accurately estimate my own fixed-cost floor?" Pull three months of actual bank and card statements and separate every transaction into "would exist even if I lost all discretionary flexibility this month" versus everything else. This takes an hour, not a full financial planning session, and it's considerably more accurate than a guess. If a specific cost is genuinely ambiguous — a phone plan, a modest gym membership tied to a real health need — err toward including it in the floor if removing it would create a real hardship, and toward excluding it if removing it would just be mildly unpleasant. The test doesn't need to be perfect to be enormously more useful than skipping it entirely.

The two failure modes, side by side

It's worth stating both failure modes plainly, next to each other, because most discussion of savings rates only ever addresses one of them — usually the first, because it's the one that produces visible distress. A flat rate that's too high for a given floor produces a savings plan that fails repeatedly, gets manually disabled, and leaves the saver blaming their own discipline for what was actually a math problem from the start. A flat rate that's too low for a given floor produces a savings plan that never fails at all — it just quietly under-delivers for decades, with no visible moment where anything goes wrong, which is exactly why it's so rarely caught or corrected. Both failures cost real money and real time. Only one of them announces itself.

Frequently misunderstood point: the floor isn't a survival minimum

A common misreading of the fixed-cost floor test treats it as an exercise in austerity — strip everything down to the bare legal minimum required to stay housed and fed, then call whatever's left the gap. That's not what Step 1 is asking for, and applying it that way produces a floor that's dishonest in the opposite direction from an inflated one, and just as useless. A floor built on bare-minimum groceries that no one could actually sustain for a full month, or a insurance choice that leaves a household genuinely exposed to a cost that would blow through any buffer the first time it's needed, isn't a more rigorous floor. It's a floor that will get violated within a few months, at which point the entire gap calculation built on top of it collapses along with it.

The floor should reflect a genuinely sustainable, realistic version of covering the essentials — the version you could actually live inside for years without quiet resentment building against the plan itself. This distinction matters because a savings rate calculated against an artificially punitive floor produces a gap that looks larger than it actually is, which in turn produces a savings rate that looks more impressive on paper than it is in practice, right up until the household can't sustain the underlying floor and the whole structure needs a redo. An honest floor, even a generous one within reason, produces a savings rate that actually holds.

A short exercise: calculating your own floor and gap right now

Before moving to Chapter 2's bracket math, it's worth actually running Chapter 1's test against your own numbers rather than reading the worked examples and mentally substituting your own income without doing the real arithmetic. Pull your last three months of bank and card statements. For each transaction, ask one question: would this still exist, at roughly this amount, if every discretionary dollar in the household disappeared this month? Housing, insurance premiums, a realistic grocery baseline, minimum debt payments, utilities, and necessary transportation costs almost always answer yes. Dining out, subscriptions beyond a genuine necessity, upgraded versions of things a cheaper version would also satisfy, and anything explicitly optional almost always answer no.

Total the "yes" column across the three months and divide by three to get a stable monthly floor, smoothing out any single month's noise. Subtract that floor from your average monthly take-home income to get your gap. Write both numbers down somewhere you'll actually see again — Chapter 2 uses this exact pair of numbers to place you in a bracket and calculate a starting rate, and Chapter 9's full sequence assumes you already have them in hand rather than needing to derive them from scratch in the middle of a longer calculation.

What to do if the exercise produces a negative or near-zero gap

Occasionally this exercise produces a gap that's negative or effectively zero — take-home income that doesn't fully cover even an honestly calculated floor. This is a real and serious finding, and it deserves a direct answer rather than being folded into the same "start small" guidance that applies to a thin-but-positive gap. A negative or near-zero gap means no percentage of it, however small, produces a meaningful, sustainable savings rate, because there's genuinely nothing left to work with once the floor is covered. In this specific situation, the honest next step isn't a smaller savings target — it's directing effort at the two things that can actually move a negative gap toward a positive one: reducing the floor itself (a real, if often difficult, look at housing costs, insurance shopping, or other genuinely negotiable fixed costs), or increasing income. Chapter 3's debt-focused math and Chapter 2's bracket table won't produce a useful number against a gap that isn't there yet — they become useful the moment the floor and income work has moved the gap into positive territory, however modest.

A third worked example: renting versus owning, and why the floor test doesn't care which

A common objection to the fixed-cost floor test is that it treats housing as a single line item without distinguishing between renting and owning, when the two involve genuinely different financial structures — a mortgage payment builds equity, a rent payment doesn't. It's worth addressing directly, because the distinction matters for a household's overall net worth but doesn't actually change how the floor test itself should treat the payment.

Consider two households with identical take-home income of $5,400 a month. The first rents at $1,900 a month. The second owns, with a mortgage payment (principal, interest, taxes, and insurance combined) of $1,900 a month — the same dollar figure, coincidentally, though the underlying math would hold at any comparable figure. For the purposes of the floor test in this chapter, both households include the full $1,900 in their fixed-cost floor, because in both cases, that $1,900 is money that has to leave the household every month regardless of any savings decision — it's not available to be redirected toward the gap. The fact that the homeowner's payment is partially building equity doesn't make that portion of the payment available for other spending; it's still committed, still due, still part of the floor exactly as the renter's payment is.

Where the distinction matters is in a separate calculation entirely — total net worth growth, which the homeowner's equity contributes to independently of their calculated savings rate. A homeowner directing $646 a month to savings per this chapter's method is, in a real sense, building wealth through two channels simultaneously: the calculated savings rate, and the equity portion of their housing payment, which a renter's identical housing cost doesn't provide. This isn't a reason to shrink the homeowner's floor to "reward" them with a larger gap — the equity-building effect is already happening independently, off to the side of the floor-and-gap calculation, and folding it into the floor test would double-count a benefit that's better tracked separately, through simple net-worth statements that include home equity as its own line item. The floor test in this chapter answers one specific question — how much is genuinely available above fixed costs to allocate toward savings — and a mortgage's equity-building quality, real and valuable as it is, doesn't change the answer to that specific question.

Frequently misunderstood point: the gap isn't the same as "money left over at the end of the month"

A subtle but important distinction separates this chapter's gap from the more familiar, informal idea of "whatever's left over at the end of the month" that most people already track loosely, often without any formal method at all. The gap, as this chapter defines it, is a calculated figure — income minus an honestly estimated fixed-cost floor — arrived at deliberately, before any spending happens. "What's left over" is an after-the-fact residual, discovered only once a month's actual spending has already occurred, and it inherits every bit of the erosion problem this book's opening pages described: spending tends to expand to consume whatever's available, which means "what's left over" at month's end is frequently a much smaller, much less reliable number than the gap this chapter's method calculates in advance.

This distinction is the entire reason the fixed-cost floor test asks you to calculate the floor deliberately, from real statements, rather than simply watching what a typical month leaves behind. A household that waits to see what's left over at the end of the month, rather than calculating the gap directly and treating the resulting savings rate as a fixed, upfront allocation, is quietly reverting to exactly the residual-savings pattern this book's opening chapter identified as the core mechanical failure behind most under-saving — savings treated as whatever remains after everything else has already happened, rather than as a deliberate allocation decided in advance. The gap calculated in this chapter is meant to feed directly into an upfront, automatic transfer, of the kind this library's companion volume on automation builds out in full — not into a passive habit of checking a balance at month's end and calling whatever remains "savings."

Setting up the rest of this book

Every chapter that follows this one assumes you've calculated, or are willing to calculate, your own fixed-cost floor and your own gap. That single number — the gap between your take-home income and your true floor — is the foundation the rest of this book's math is built on, in the same way account architecture is the load-bearing piece of this library's companion volume on automation. Chapter 2 uses the gap to build out real, worked savings-rate math across several income brackets. Chapter 3 adjusts the gap-based rate for high-interest debt sitting on top of it. Every later chapter assumes the floor test as a starting calculation, not a one-time exercise — it's worth recalculating any time your fixed costs or income shift meaningfully, which several later chapters address directly, particularly the life-transition math in Chapter 4.

Chapter 2 — Savings Rate by Income Bracket, With Real Math

The situation

A reader who's internalized Chapter 1's fixed-cost floor test has a fair follow-up question: fine, the flat percentage is wrong, but what number should actually replace it? Knowing that the rate should scale with the gap between income and the floor is useful in principle, but it doesn't yet answer, in concrete numbers, what a sustainable rate actually looks like for someone at a specific point on the income spectrum. This chapter answers that question directly, with real math worked through at several representative brackets, so the abstract framework from Chapter 1 becomes a set of numbers you can actually compare your own situation against.

The mechanics

The relationship between a household's gap and its sustainable savings percentage isn't linear, and understanding why matters before looking at the specific brackets. As the gap widens relative to income, the marginal value of discretionary spending — the value of the next dollar spent on something beyond the floor — tends to decline faster than the marginal value of saving that same dollar. A household whose gap is small genuinely needs most of that gap for real quality-of-life spending: the occasional dinner out, a birthday gift, a small buffer against an unplanned cost that doesn't fully break the floor. A household whose gap is large has already covered all of that flexible spending many times over with a much smaller fraction of their gap, and additional discretionary spending past that point buys progressively less genuine well-being per dollar — a phenomenon covered in more depth in Chapter 8's discussion of diminishing returns, but worth flagging here because it's the underlying reason the sustainable *percentage of the gap* rises as the gap itself grows, rather than staying flat.

This produces something like a rising marginal savings rate — not unlike a progressive tax bracket, but running in the opposite direction: the more room a household has above its floor, the higher a percentage of that additional room can sustainably go to savings without meaningfully reducing genuine quality of life. This is the mechanism that explains why the second household in Chapter 1's opening example could comfortably push their savings rate well past a flat 20% of income while the first household, if forced to the same standard, would have had to cut into essentials to get there.

The framework: bracket math

The brackets below are organized by the ratio between a household's gap and their total take-home income — not by income alone, since (as Chapter 1's second worked example showed) two households at the same income can sit in different brackets depending on their actual floor. For each bracket, a sustainable range for the *percentage of the gap* directed to savings is given, along with what that typically translates to as a percentage of total income, so you can see both figures side by side.

Bracket 1 — Gap under 15% of income. This is a household whose fixed costs consume the overwhelming majority of take-home pay, often (though not always) at lower absolute income levels, though a household with high fixed costs relative to a moderate income can land here too. A sustainable savings rate against a gap this thin is typically 10 to

20% of the gap — small in absolute terms, and correctly so, because most of the remaining room needs to stay available for real, unavoidable discretionary needs and a thin margin of error. As a percentage of total income, this typically works out to somewhere under 3%. This is not a failing number. It's an honest one, and Chapter 4's approach to raising it as circumstances change is the correct next step, not a larger flat target imposed immediately.

Bracket 2 — Gap between 15% and 35% of income. This is a household with a genuine but moderate cushion above their floor — enough room that discretionary spending doesn't feel punishing, but not so much that saving aggressively goes unnoticed. A sustainable rate here typically runs 25 to 40% of the gap, translating to roughly 5 to 12% of total income depending on exactly where within the bracket the household sits. This is the bracket where a household is likely to still feel some real tension between saving more and spending on quality of life — a tension that's appropriate at this level, not a sign anything's being done wrong.

Bracket 3 — Gap between 35% and 55% of income. Here the household has a substantial cushion, and the sustainable percentage of the gap rises accordingly, typically to somewhere between 40 and 55%. As a percentage of total income, this often lands in a range that comfortably exceeds the commonly cited 20% flat benchmark — often somewhere between 15 and 28% of total income — without requiring any real sacrifice in day-to-day discretionary spending, because the gap itself is large enough to absorb a higher percentage while still leaving meaningful room for lifestyle.

Bracket 4 — Gap above 55% of income. A household this far above its floor has, in a very real sense, more money than its actual cost of living requires to sustain a genuinely comfortable lifestyle. A sustainable rate against a gap this size often runs 50 to 65% of the gap, which frequently translates to 30% or more of total income — a figure that would sound aggressive against a flat-percentage framework but is, against this household's actual floor, entirely sustainable without meaningful lifestyle compromise. Chapter 8's ceiling discussion becomes especially relevant at this bracket, since the question shifts from "can this household afford to save more" (almost always yes) to "does saving significantly more than this actually serve their goals" (a genuinely open question worth calculating rather than assuming).

Worked example

Take three households, each earning a different income, each with the fixed-cost floor calculated using Chapter 1's method.

Household A earns $3,100 a month take-home with a floor of $2,700, a gap of $400 (roughly 13% of income) — Bracket 1. A sustainable rate of 15% of the gap is $60 a month, or about 2% of income. Small, but real, automatable, and sustainable through a bad month without breaking.

Household B earns $6,400 a month take-home with a floor of $4,600, a gap of $1,800 (28% of income) — Bracket 2. A sustainable rate of 32% of the gap is $576 a month, or 9% of income — already meaningfully more thoughtful than a flat 20%-of-income target would have demanded ($1,280), and considerably more sustainable to maintain without erosion.

Household C earns $14,200 a month take-home with a floor of $6,300, a gap of $7,900 (56% of income) — Bracket 4. A sustainable rate of 55% of the gap is $4,345 a month, or roughly 31% of income — well above the flat 20% benchmark ($2,840), capturing an additional $1,505 a month, or over $18,000 a year, that a flat rule would have left unclaimed.

None of these three households is doing anything wrong relative to a flat rule that asked all three for 20% of income. Household A couldn't have hit it without cutting into their floor. Household C could have hit it in their sleep and still had enormous room left unclaimed. Only the bracket math, built on each household's actual gap, produces a number that's simultaneously sustainable for Household A and sufficiently ambitious for Household C.

Recalculating your bracket as your gap changes

A household's bracket isn't fixed for life — it shifts every time income or fixed costs move meaningfully, and the sustainable rate should shift with it rather than staying anchored to whatever bracket applied when the plan was first set. A raise widens the gap and can move a household from Bracket 2 into Bracket 3, at which point the sustainable percentage of the gap rises, not just the absolute dollar amount tracking a fixed percentage. A move to a lower-cost area with the same income has the identical effect, shrinking the floor and widening the gap without any change in pay at all. This chapter's brackets aren't a one-time classification — they're worth recalculating at least annually, or any time a major change hits either side of the gap equation, using the same fixed-cost floor test from Chapter 1.

A note on how these brackets interact with debt and life transitions

The bracket math in this chapter assumes a household with no unusual debt burden and no active life transition underway — a genuinely useful baseline, but one that two later chapters modify directly. A household otherwise sitting in Bracket 3 but carrying meaningful high-interest debt should read Chapter 3 before finalizing a rate, since debt changes not just the amount saved but where a portion of that gap should be directed instead. A household mid-transition — a new baby, a home purchase, a career change — should read Chapter 4 before treating their current bracket as a stable, long-term classification, since several common transitions temporarily shrink the gap in ways this chapter's baseline math doesn't yet account for. The bracket framework in this chapter is the foundation the rest of the book adjusts, not a final answer on its own for every household.

Common objections and how to handle them

"These brackets still feel like another flat rule, just with more steps." The difference is what the percentage is calculated against. A flat rule applies one number to income, ignoring the floor entirely. This chapter's brackets apply a rising percentage to the gap specifically, which means two households at the same income but different floors land in different brackets and get different, individually correct numbers — something a single flat percentage can never produce, no matter how many tiers it adds, unless it's also tracking each household's floor.

"What if my gap sits right at a bracket boundary?" Treat the percentage ranges as continuous rather than as hard steps — a gap sitting at 34% of income, just under the Bracket 3 threshold, doesn't need to be treated identically to a gap at 16%;

it's reasonable to lean toward the higher end of Bracket 2's range in that case. The brackets are a practical simplification of what is, underneath, a smooth relationship between gap size and sustainable savings percentage — useful for quick orientation, not a rigid cutoff that changes everything at one exact number.

"Do these numbers hold regardless of household size?" The floor calculation from Chapter 1 already accounts for household size implicitly, since a larger household has a larger real fixed-cost floor — more groceries, more space, potentially childcare. Once the floor reflects the actual household, the bracket math applies the same way regardless of how many people that floor is supporting. What changes across household sizes is the floor itself, not the logic connecting gap size to sustainable savings percentage.

A second worked example: the same bracket math applied to a raise

A worker earning $5,200 a month take-home with a floor of $4,000 sits in Bracket 2, gap of $1,200 (23% of income), with a sustainable rate around 30% of the gap — $360 a month, or roughly 7% of income. A year later, a promotion raises take-home pay to $6,800 a month while the floor rises only modestly, to $4,300, since housing and insurance didn't jump proportionally with the raise. The new gap is $2,500, now 37% of income — crossing into Bracket 3. The sustainable rate rises accordingly, to somewhere around 42% of the new gap: $1,050 a month, or roughly 15% of the new income. This is the bracket math doing exactly what a flat percentage never could — not just scaling the dollar amount up with the raise, but recognizing that the *type* of household this now is has genuinely changed, and adjusting the underlying percentage, not just the number it's applied to.

A third worked example: a two-income household

Bracket math doesn't require collapsing two incomes into a single undifferentiated household figure before it becomes useful, and it's worth showing how it applies when a household has two earners with different incomes rather than one. Consider two partners earning $3,900 and $2,600 a month take-home respectively, a combined $6,500, with a shared fixed-cost floor of $4,700 covering rent, groceries, insurance, and utilities for the household as a whole. The combined gap is $1,800, or 28%

of combined income — Bracket 2, with a sustainable rate around 32% of the gap: $576 a month.

The bracket calculation itself doesn't care whether that $576 comes from one earner or is split between both, but the household still has to decide how to divide it, and there are two defensible approaches to choose between deliberately rather than defaulting to whichever feels easiest in the moment. An even split ($288 each) is simple but ignores that the two incomes aren't equal, meaning the lower earner is contributing a noticeably larger share of their own personal income than the higher earner is. A proportional split, matching each partner's contribution to their share of total income (60% from the higher earner, 40% from the lower, or $346 and $230 respectively) keeps the burden proportionate to each person's actual earning capacity, which tends to feel more equitable in practice and avoids one partner's discretionary room shrinking disproportionately relative to the other's. Neither approach changes the household's total bracket-based rate — the $576 figure is fixed by the combined floor-and-gap math regardless of how it's split — but the split itself is a real decision worth making deliberately rather than defaulting to an even division that quietly asks more, proportionally, of the lower earner every single month.

A short exercise: placing yourself in a bracket

Using the floor and gap you calculated at the end of Chapter 1, divide your gap by your total take-home income to get a single ratio, expressed as a percentage. Compare that percentage against the four bracket thresholds in this chapter — under 15%, 15 to 35%, 35 to 55%, above 55% — to find your current bracket. Then apply the midpoint of that bracket's suggested percentage-of-gap range to your own gap to get a first-pass sustainable rate. This isn't a final number — Chapters 3 through 8 each cover situations that might adjust it further, and Chapter 9 walks through the full sequence for combining every relevant adjustment — but it's a genuinely useful starting figure, calculated from your own real numbers rather than borrowed from anyone else's, and considerably more informative than a flat percentage that was never built with your floor in mind at all.

Frequently misunderstood point: brackets aren't a judgment of the household, they're a description of the math

It's easy to read the bracket labels in this chapter — a household with a thin gap sitting in Bracket 1, a household with a wide one sitting in Bracket 4 — as some kind of implicit ranking of financial success, with Bracket 4 as the "winning" position everyone should be working toward. That reading misses what the brackets are actually describing. A household's bracket is a direct mathematical consequence of the relationship between their income and their true fixed-cost floor in their specific location, at their specific stage of life — not a measure of effort, intelligence, or financial virtue. A nurse working nights in a high-cost city and a software engineer working remotely from a low-cost town can have similar effort and similar financial discipline while landing in entirely different brackets, purely because their floors and incomes produce different gaps.

This distinction matters practically, not just as a fairness point, because misreading the brackets as a moral ranking produces exactly the same guilt-and-shame dynamic this book's opening chapter was written to dismantle in the first place — just relocated from a single flat percentage to a four-tier system instead of a one-tier one. The brackets exist to produce an accurate, achievable number for wherever a household actually sits, not to sort households into a hierarchy of financial adequacy. A Bracket 1 household following this chapter's math correctly, saving a small but genuinely sustainable amount every month, is doing exactly as well by this book's standard as a Bracket 4 household saving a much larger dollar figure — both are running the correct calculation for their own gap, which is the only standard either chapter or this book is actually applying.

A note on how brackets interact with cost-of-living differences within the same country

Two readers in the same income bracket by raw dollar figures can experience very different real brackets once their local cost of living is factored in, and it's worth being explicit that this chapter's math is built to handle that automatically, provided the floor calculation from Chapter 1 was done honestly and locally rather than borrowed from a national average. A

$70,000 salary supports a dramatically different floor, and therefore a dramatically different gap and bracket, in a high-cost coastal city than it does in a lower-cost inland region — sometimes different enough to place otherwise-identical earners two full brackets apart. This isn't a flaw in the bracket system; it's the entire reason the bracket math is calculated from each household's own floor rather than from a lookup table keyed to income alone. A national average savings benchmark, of the kind flagged as a reasonable comparison point but not a target in Chapter 1, runs into exactly this problem — it can't account for local cost differences the way a floor calculated at the individual household level automatically does.

A note on published percentile benchmarks and how they relate to this chapter's brackets

Independent research sources — including the Federal Reserve's periodic Survey of Consumer Finances and Vanguard's annual "How America Saves" report — publish real, aggregated data on how much actual households at various income and age percentiles are saving in practice. It's worth being precise about how this kind of published percentile data relates to the bracket math in this chapter, because the two are answering genuinely different questions and shouldn't be confused with each other.

A percentile benchmark answers a descriptive question: given real, observed behavior across a large sample, what does a typical household at a given income or age actually save. This chapter's bracket math answers a prescriptive question: given a specific household's own floor and gap, what *should* that household sustainably save. These can diverge meaningfully, in either direction — a percentile benchmark reflects the same flat-percentage instincts, uneven financial literacy, and varying local costs that this book's opening chapter argues produce systematically wrong outcomes for many households, which means "typical" behavior in a percentile dataset isn't the same as "correctly calculated" behavior under this book's method. A household that discovers their own bracket-calculated rate sits well above the reported percentile for their income and age isn't necessarily over-saving; a household whose bracket-calculated rate sits below the reported percentile isn't necessarily under-saving. Both comparisons are worth noting out of curiosity, but neither should override a rate that's been calculated directly from a household's own real floor and gap using this chapter's method — the percentile data describes what other households are actually doing, not what any specific household's own numbers support.

A fourth worked example: a household that moves between brackets over a single decade

To show the bracket math functioning as a live, recalculated tool rather than a single static classification, it's useful to trace one household across several genuine shifts over a ten-year stretch, rather than a single before-and-after snapshot. At year one, a household earns $4,400 a month take-home against a floor of $3,700, a thin Bracket 1 gap of $700, with a sustainable rate around $105 a month — modest, and correctly so, for a household this close to its floor.

By year three, a combination of a modest raise and a slightly lower floor (a car loan paid off, freeing up its monthly payment) widens the gap to $1,450, crossing into Bracket 2, with a sustainable rate rising to roughly $420 a month. By year six, a larger promotion pushes take-home to $7,100 while the floor grows only modestly to $4,200 (a somewhat larger home, but not a proportional jump with the raise), producing a gap of $2,900 — solidly in Bracket 3, with a sustainable rate around $1,247 a month. By year eight, the household has a child, and per Chapter 4's transition-reset framework, the floor rises to account for new childcare costs, temporarily narrowing the gap and pulling the sustainable rate back down for a defined period, before the year-ten mark sees childcare costs settle into a more predictable pattern and the gap widen again as the temporary transition resolves.

Across this same decade, the household's savings rate as a raw dollar figure moved from $105 to $420 to $1,247, dipped during the year-eight transition, and rose again by year ten — not because the household became more or less disciplined at any point along the way, but because their bracket, calculated fresh at each meaningful shift in income or floor, genuinely changed multiple times. A flat percentage applied across this same decade would have produced a single, unchanging fraction of income throughout, missing every one of these real shifts entirely — either asking too much in year one, too little by year six, or failing to account for the temporary transition in year eight at all. The bracket math, recalculated at each real shift, tracked the household's actual situation the entire way through, which is the whole argument this chapter and Chapter 9's closing sequence are built to make concrete.

Chapter 3 — Adjusting for High-Interest Debt Already in the Picture

The situation

Someone carrying $16,000 in credit card debt at an interest rate around 24% APR is told, by the same flat-rule advice covered in the first two chapters, to save 20% of their income. They dutifully split their available money between minimum debt payments and a savings transfer, and eighteen months later they've accumulated a small savings balance while the credit card balance has barely moved — interest has been consuming most of what should have been progress. They've technically followed the advice. The math underneath it was working against them the entire time.

The mechanics

This is a math problem with a genuinely correct answer, not a matter of preference or discipline, and it's worth stating plainly before anything else: paying down debt at a high interest rate is mathematically equivalent to earning a guaranteed return equal to that interest rate, because every dollar directed at the balance stops that specific rate from accruing on that specific dollar going forward. A credit card at 24% APR means every dollar of principal paid down is a dollar that would otherwise have cost 24% annually in interest — a guaranteed, risk-free return no investment account can reliably promise. Compare that to typical long-run stock market returns, which have historically averaged somewhere in the high single digits to low double digits annually over long periods, with real years of loss mixed in along the way, and the comparison isn't close. A guaranteed 24% return beats an uncertain roughly 8 to 10% return in almost every realistic scenario, and it beats it by a wide enough margin that "split it evenly" is usually the wrong instinct even though it feels balanced and reasonable.

This doesn't mean debt payoff should always take 100% of a household's available gap, and it's worth being precise about the two real exceptions, both of which matter enough to change the math. First, an employer retirement match is close to a guaranteed, immediate return that frequently exceeds even a high-interest debt rate once the match percentage is annualized against the contribution required to get it — walking away from a full employer match to pay down debt faster is very often leaving free money on the table that no debt payoff, however high the interest rate, can match. Second, a household with zero liquid buffer is one unplanned expense away from taking on *new* high-interest debt to cover it, which can undo months of payoff progress in a single event — a minimal starter buffer, even a small one, is worth maintaining before directing everything at high-interest debt, covered in more depth in the account-architecture side of this library's companion volume.

Below the employer match and a minimal starter buffer, though, the math strongly favors weighting the available gap heavily toward high-interest debt rather than splitting it evenly with savings, for exactly the reason above: the guaranteed return on payoff beats the uncertain return on most other savings destinations, for any debt carrying an interest rate meaningfully above what a diversified long-term investment could realistically be expected to return.

The framework: the rate-threshold split

Step 1 — Always capture any full employer retirement match first, regardless of other debt. If an employer match requires a specific contribution percentage to fully capture, that percentage comes off the top of the gap before anything else, because its effective return typically exceeds even high-interest debt once matched dollars are annualized against the contribution needed to unlock them.

Step 2 — Build or maintain a minimal starter buffer before weighting heavily toward debt. This isn't the full three-to-six-month buffer covered elsewhere in this library — it's a smaller, faster target, often in the range of one month of the fixed-cost floor calculated in Chapter 1, sized specifically to prevent a single unplanned expense from becoming new high-interest debt while payoff is underway.

Step 3 — Compare each remaining debt's interest rate against a realistic long-run investment return threshold, commonly somewhere around 7 to 9%. Debt above that threshold should receive the large majority of the remaining gap — commonly 80% or more — because the guaranteed return from payoff outperforms the uncertain return from saving or investing the same dollar. Debt below that threshold (a low-rate auto loan, a subsidized student loan, a mortgage) doesn't carry the same urgency, and the gap can be split more evenly between continued minimum payments on that lower-rate debt and normal saving per the bracket math from Chapter 2.

Step 4 — Recalculate your bracket from Chapter 2 using the *post-debt* gap once high-interest debt is cleared. The percentage that had been going to high-interest payoff doesn't need to be renegotiated from scratch — it simply becomes available to redirect into the bracket-based savings rate that would otherwise apply, now working with a larger effective gap since a former debt payment has disappeared from the fixed-cost floor.

Worked example

A household with a $6,800 monthly take-home, a fixed-cost floor of $5,100 (including minimum payments on all debt), and a gap of $1,700 is carrying $16,000 in credit card debt at 24% APR, alongside a low-rate auto loan already folded into the floor. They have no employer match available and a starter buffer already in place from an earlier period.

Applying the rate-threshold split, since the credit card sits well above the roughly 8% investment-return threshold, the household directs 85% of their $1,700 gap — $1,445 a month — to extra payments on the credit card, with the remaining $255 continuing to build general savings per Bracket 2 math from Chapter 2. At this payoff rate, the $16,000 balance clears in just under twelve months, factoring in the declining interest as the balance shrinks. Compare this to an even 50/50 split of the same gap: $850 a month to the card would have taken close to twenty months to clear the same balance, because a slower payoff rate means more months of that 24% rate compounding against a larger remaining balance the whole way through — a difference of roughly eight additional months during which most of each smaller payment was still going to interest rather than principal.

Once the card clears at month twelve, the household's fixed-cost floor drops (the minimum payment that had been baked into it disappears), which widens their gap. Recalculating their bracket from Chapter 2 with this new, larger gap produces a higher sustainable general savings rate than they had before the debt was ever incurred — not because their income changed, but because a dollar that used to service 24% interest is now available to compound in their own favor instead.

A second worked example: multiple debts at different rates

A different household carries three debts simultaneously: a credit card at 22% APR with a $4,200 balance, a personal loan at 11% APR with a $7,500 balance, and a car loan at 5.5% APR with a $9,000 balance, already included in their fixed-cost floor via its minimum payment. Their available gap, after minimums on all three and Step 1's employer match capture, is $900 a month.

Applying the rate-threshold split against a roughly 8% investment-return benchmark: the credit card at 22% and the personal loan at 11% both sit above the threshold and both warrant aggressive extra payment, while the car loan at 5.5% sits below it and doesn't need extra payment beyond its already-included minimum. Within the two debts above the threshold, the higher rate gets priority — this is the same debt-avalanche logic covered in this library's dedicated debt-payoff volume, and this book doesn't re-derive that ordering mechanic in full; what this chapter adds is the *savings-rate* question sitting on top of it. The household directs the full $900 toward the credit card first, clearing it in roughly five months, then redirects that $900 to the personal loan, clearing it faster than its original schedule alone would have allowed. Only once both above-threshold debts are cleared does the freed-up $900 shift into the bracket-based general savings rate from Chapter 2, now calculated against a meaningfully larger gap than the household started with.

Addressing the obvious objection: "shouldn't I save something the whole time, even during aggressive payoff?"

This is a fair concern, and the framework in this chapter already answers it through Step 2's minimal starter buffer — the point isn't to save literally nothing while carrying high-interest debt, it's to weight the split heavily rather than evenly, for the specific mathematical reason covered above. A household that feels uneasy directing 80% or more of their gap to debt payoff, even with a starter buffer in place, isn't wrong to want more of a cushion — but it's worth being honest about the cost of that comfort: every month of a softer split is a month of continued high-rate interest accruing on a larger remaining balance, and that cost compounds in the wrong direction the same way savings compound in the right one. A reasonable middle ground for someone who needs the psychological comfort of visibly growing savings during payoff is a 70/30 split rather than 85/15, accepting a somewhat longer payoff timeline in exchange for a faster-growing visible savings balance — a real tradeoff, made consciously, rather than an even split chosen by default because it feels fair without actually being examined against the math.

What counts as "high interest" in this framework

The roughly 7 to 9% threshold used throughout this chapter isn't an arbitrary round number — it approximates a realistic, historically grounded expectation for long-run diversified investment returns, which is the actual alternative use of the same dollar. Debt carrying an interest rate below this threshold — most mortgages, many federal student loans, many auto loans, some personal loans with strong credit — doesn't carry the same mathematical urgency, because the guaranteed "return" from paying it down early doesn't clearly beat the expected return from investing the same dollar instead, and for debt with real tax advantages (mortgage interest deductions in some circumstances, certain student loan structures), the effective comparison can tilt even further toward not accelerating payoff. This is a genuinely different situation from the high-interest case this chapter focuses on, and treating every debt identically — either always prioritizing payoff over saving, or always prioritizing saving over payoff — misses the actual math in both directions. The threshold, not the mere existence of debt, is what should drive the split.

What about 0% promotional-rate debt

A specific case worth addressing on its own: debt carrying a genuine 0% promotional interest rate for a fixed introductory period — a balance transfer offer, a promotional financing plan on a large purchase — behaves very differently from the high-interest case this chapter is otherwise built around, and treating it identically would be a mistake in the opposite direction. While the 0% period genuinely holds, there's no guaranteed return being forfeited by *not* accelerating payoff, since no interest is accruing to avoid. In this specific window, it's often mathematically sound to make only the minimum payment on the 0% balance and direct the freed-up gap toward the bracket-based savings rate from Chapter 2 instead, effectively using an interest-free loan as working capital while the terms allow it.

The real risk with 0% promotional debt isn't the rate itself — it's the transition at the end of the promotional period, when the rate typically reverts to a standard, often high, ongoing rate, sometimes applied retroactively to the full original balance under some card agreements if the balance isn't cleared in time. The correct approach is to treat the 0% balance as a debt with a hard deadline: calculate the monthly payment required to clear the full balance before the promotional period ends, and treat that specific number as a fixed, non-negotiable floor addition for the duration of the promotional window, separate from and prior to any other savings-rate calculation in this chapter. Only gap remaining after that calculated payoff-by-deadline amount should be split using the rest of this chapter's framework or directed toward Chapter 2's general bracket math. Missing the deadline converts what looked like free financing into exactly the high-interest case this chapter's core framework is built to handle — at which point the standard rate-threshold split applies in full, against whatever balance remains.

A short exercise: the rate-threshold test on your own debt

List every debt you're currently carrying, with its exact interest rate, in a single column. Next to each, write "above threshold" or "below threshold" using the roughly 7 to 9% range from this chapter as your dividing line, adjusted slightly based on your own read of realistic long-run investment returns if you have a more specific figure you trust. For every debt marked "above threshold," rank them from highest rate to lowest — this is the order extra payments should flow once Step 1 and Step 2's employer-match and starter-buffer priorities are satisfied. For every debt marked "below threshold," set them aside from this chapter's aggressive-payoff logic entirely; they continue on their standard minimum-payment schedule and don't compete with your bracket-based savings rate from Chapter 2 for any of your gap. This single sorting exercise, done once and updated whenever a new debt is taken on or an old one clears, removes the guesswork from what would otherwise be a recurring, emotionally loaded decision every time there's extra money to allocate.

A note on the psychological cost of an aggressive payoff split

This chapter's math is unambiguous about the numbers, but it's worth acknowledging directly that an 80-or-more-percent split toward debt payoff carries a real, non-financial cost that a purely mathematical framework can understate: the feeling of having almost nothing visible accumulating in savings for months at a stretch, even while real financial progress is happening in the form of a shrinking balance. This isn't a reason to abandon the math — the household in this chapter's second worked example clears two debts nearly a year faster than an even split would have allowed, a genuinely large difference — but it is a reason to build in a specific, deliberate counterweight rather than assuming pure numerical optimality will feel sustainable in practice for every household.

One practical counterweight: track and display debt payoff progress with the same visibility a savings account balance normally gets — a simple chart or running total of the shrinking balance, checked on the same schedule a savings account might be checked, so the household has a concrete, visible number moving in the right direction even though that number represents debt eliminated rather than dollars accumulated. Households that skip this step sometimes report the aggressive-payoff period feeling worse than the math alone would predict, purely because there was nothing satisfying to look at along the way — a solvable problem, not a flaw in the underlying framework.

A second short exercise: projecting your own payoff timeline

Using the debt list from the exercise above, and the specific split this chapter recommends (roughly 80% or more of the available gap, after Step 1 and Step 2, directed at above-threshold debt in rate order), estimate your own payoff timeline for each above-threshold debt using any reputable, free debt-payoff calculator. Compare that timeline against what an even 50/50 split between debt and general savings would produce for the same debts. The gap between the two timelines — often, as in this chapter's worked examples, a difference of many months — is the concrete, dollar-and-time cost of treating debt payoff and savings as equally weighted competitors for the same gap, rather than applying the rate-threshold logic this chapter is built around.

A note on consolidation and refinancing as a separate lever from the savings-rate split

Debt consolidation and refinancing — combining several debts into a single new loan, or replacing an existing debt with a new one at a lower rate — are real tools worth understanding, and it's worth being clear about how they relate to this chapter's framework rather than treating them as a substitute for it. A successful consolidation or refinance lowers the effective interest rate on a debt, which can shift that debt from "above threshold" to "below threshold" in the rate-threshold split from this chapter, changing how aggressively it should be prioritized relative to general saving. A household that refinances a 22% credit card balance into a 9% personal loan hasn't paid off the debt, but they have meaningfully changed which side of this chapter's threshold it falls on, and the correct savings-rate split should be recalculated against the new, lower rate rather than the original one.

This is a genuinely different lever from anything this chapter's core framework adjusts directly — the rate-threshold split takes a debt's interest rate as a given and calculates the correct allocation around it; consolidation and refinancing change the rate itself, before the allocation math ever runs. Worth flagging directly: a consolidation that lowers the monthly payment by extending the repayment term, without meaningfully lowering the total interest rate, doesn't accomplish the same thing — it can make a debt feel more manageable month to month while actually increasing the total interest paid over the life of the loan, since more months means more time for interest to accrue even at an unchanged or only slightly lower rate. Before treating any consolidation or refinance offer as a reason to recalculate this chapter's split, confirm that the new arrangement genuinely lowers the effective rate, not just the monthly payment.

A note on debt taken on for an appreciating or income-generating purpose

Everything in this chapter's threshold logic assumes debt that's purely a cost — a credit card balance, a personal loan for consumption — with no offsetting asset or income attached to it. It's worth addressing directly a different case: debt taken on specifically to acquire an appreciating asset or to fund something that itself generates income, such as a loan used to purchase equipment for a income-generating side business, or debt tied to an investment property rather than a primary residence. This category doesn't fit cleanly into either side of this chapter's threshold, because the debt's true cost isn't just its stated interest rate — it's the interest rate net of whatever return the debt itself is helping to generate.

The correct approach for this specific category: calculate a net effective rate by subtracting the reasonably expected return or income the debt is helping produce from its stated interest rate, and apply this chapter's threshold test to that net figure rather than the raw stated rate. A loan at 9% used to purchase equipment reasonably expected to generate a return well above that rate has a genuinely different urgency than a 9% personal loan funding pure consumption with no offsetting return at all, even though the two carry an identical stated interest rate. This calculation requires real honesty about the expected return, not optimistic best-case projections — an equipment purchase that might generate additional income, but isn't guaranteed to, should be evaluated using a conservative estimate of that additional income, not the most optimistic version, since an inflated expected return used to justify treating high-cost debt as low-priority is exactly the kind of self-serving math this chapter's threshold test exists to prevent.

Chapter 4 — Savings Rate During Major Life Transitions

The situation

A household that had settled into a comfortable, well-calculated savings rate — built using the bracket math from Chapter 2, tested and sustained for over a year — has a baby. Six months later, they're quietly panicking, because the rate that used to feel effortless now bounces some months and barely clears in others, and they're interpreting this as a failure of discipline or planning rather than what it actually is: a genuine, temporary shift in their fixed-cost floor that their savings rate hasn't caught up to yet.

This is one version of a pattern that recurs across several distinct life transitions — a new child, a home purchase, a career change or gap, a significant move — each of which temporarily reshapes the floor-and-gap math from Chapter 1 in a way that a static savings rate, calculated once and left alone, can't accommodate.

The mechanics

Every major transition covered in this chapter does one of two things to the floor-and-gap equation: it temporarily raises the floor (new recurring costs that weren't previously part of the fixed baseline), or it temporarily shrinks the gap from the income side (a career change with a pay cut, a period of reduced hours, a gap between jobs). Either mechanism produces the same downstream effect — the previously calculated savings rate, correct for the household's prior floor and gap, is now miscalibrated against a different reality, and continuing to force the old rate produces exactly the erosion-then-abandonment pattern this library's companion volume warns against: a rate that gets manually paused during a hard month and never properly restarted.

The mistake most households make during a transition isn't failing to anticipate it — many transitions, like a home purchase or a planned career change, are visible well in advance. The mistake is treating the savings rate as something that should hold steady through the transition out of a sense of discipline, rather than recalculating it deliberately for the new floor and gap, the same way Chapter 1's test would if applied fresh. A rate that held for the old reality isn't a virtue to defend through a genuinely different reality — it's simply the wrong number for a phase that's already ended.

The framework: the temporary floor reset

Step 1 — Recalculate your fixed-cost floor specifically for the transition period, not your prior baseline. A new baby typically adds a real, calculable set of recurring costs — childcare, additional health expenses, additional household costs — that belong in the floor for as long as they're genuinely fixed, not treated as discretionary spending to be trimmed around the edges. A home purchase often temporarily raises the floor through moving costs, initial furnishing, and a period of adjustment to new housing costs before the household settles into a stable pattern. A career change with a pay cut shrinks the gap from the income side rather than raising the floor, but the effect on the sustainable savings rate is mechanically identical — recalculate against the new, real numbers.

Step 2 — Recalculate your bracket and sustainable rate using Chapter 2's framework, applied to the new floor and

gap, not the old ones. This will very often mean a genuinely lower rate for the duration of the transition, and that's the correct answer, not a compromise to feel bad about. A household moving from Bracket 3 to Bracket 1 during a transition isn't backsliding — they're accurately tracking a floor that has, for the moment, genuinely grown.

Step 3 — Set an explicit, calendared review date to reassess, rather than leaving the reduced rate open-ended. Most transitions are temporary by nature — childcare costs shift as a child ages into school, a home purchase's initial costs are a one-time event rather than a permanent addition to the floor, a career change's pay cut is often recovered as the new role progresses. A reduced rate without a review date risks becoming permanent by default, the same erosion risk this chapter is designed to prevent, just running in the other direction. Three to six months out is a reasonable first checkpoint for most transitions; a genuinely long-term shift (a permanent reduction to part-time work, for instance) may need the new rate to simply become the new baseline rather than a temporary dip, decided deliberately rather than by default.

Step 4 — Resume the pre-transition rate, or move to whatever new bracket the post-transition numbers support, once the transition period genuinely ends. This is where the calendared review from Step 3 earns its value — without it, a household that could return to a higher, previously sustainable rate often simply doesn't, because there was never a deliberate moment built in to check.

Worked example: the new baby

A household previously in Bracket 3 — take-home of $8,400 a month, floor of $5,000, gap of $3,400, sustainable rate around 45% of the gap ($1,530 a month, 18% of income) — has a baby. Recalculating the floor: childcare at $1,400 a month, additional health and household costs of roughly $350 a month, brings the new floor to $6,750. Income is unchanged at $8,400, so the new gap is $1,650 — nearly halved, and now sitting in Bracket 2 rather than Bracket 3. A sustainable rate against this new gap, at roughly 32%, is $528 a month — a real reduction from $1,530, and the mathematically correct one, not a failure to sustain the old number.

The household sets a review date for month nine, when full-time daycare costs are expected to shift as care arrangements change. At that checkpoint, they recalculate the floor again — childcare costs have settled at a slightly lower, more predictable number as the family adjusts — and the gap widens back to $2,100, moving them back toward the upper end of Bracket 2, with a sustainable rate rising accordingly to around $700 a month. The rate never had to be "held" through the hardest months by force; it was correctly recalculated at each real shift in the underlying floor.

Worked example: the home purchase

A household saving toward a home down payment temporarily reallocates their entire discretionary savings gap toward that specific goal in the two years leading up to the purchase — a deliberate, goal-specific shift rather than a reduction, covered by the same bracket math applied to a single destination instead of split across several. In the three months immediately following the purchase itself, moving costs, initial furnishing, and a new, higher housing payment (even one that was fully anticipated and budgeted for) often produce a short, sharp floor increase beyond what was modeled in the pre-purchase planning — closing costs that ran slightly over estimate, an appliance that needed replacing sooner than expected, the accumulated small costs of actually moving a household. Rather than treating this three-month spike as a sign the purchase was a mistake or the budget was wrong, the household applies this chapter's framework directly: recalculate the floor for this specific short window, accept a temporarily lower or even near-zero general savings rate through it, and set a review date at the three-month mark to confirm the floor has settled back to its planned, stable post-purchase level before resuming a normal bracket-based rate.

Worked example: the career change

A worker leaving a stable role to pursue a career change takes a temporary income reduction — dropping from $6,200 to $4,800 a month take-home for roughly eighteen months while building experience in the new field, with a floor of $3,900 essentially unchanged from before. The pre-transition gap was $2,300 (Bracket 3); the new gap is $900 (Bracket 1). Rather than attempting to hold a Bracket 3 rate against Bracket 1 income — which would force cuts into the floor itself — the household deliberately drops to a Bracket 1 rate for the duration, roughly $150 a month, treating the eighteen-month window as a calculated, temporary investment in future earning capacity rather than a savings failure. A review date is set for month eighteen, aligned with the point the career change is expected to produce income growth, at which point the floor-and-gap calculation is run fresh against the new role's actual income, not the old role's, and the bracket and rate are reset from there rather than assumed to simply snap back to the pre-transition number.

Common objections and how to handle them

"Doesn't deliberately lowering my savings rate during a transition undo months or years of progress?" A temporarily lower rate doesn't touch money already saved — it only affects new contributions during the transition window, and a genuinely temporary reduction, resumed on schedule per Step 3, costs a household far less over a full working life than either forcing an unsustainable rate that eventually breaks entirely, or cutting into the floor itself to maintain appearances during a period the math simply doesn't support.

"What if the transition turns out to be longer or more expensive than planned?" Recalculate again — the framework in this chapter isn't a one-time calculation locked in at the start of the transition, it's a method to be reapplied any time the real numbers diverge meaningfully from what was planned. A career change that takes twenty-four months instead of eighteen, or a childcare cost that turns out higher than initially estimated, simply means running Step 1 and Step 2 again with updated real numbers, not abandoning the framework because the first estimate wasn't perfect.

"Should I use a buffer account to smooth over a transition instead of lowering my rate?" For a short, sharp, one-time cost — the home-purchase spike in the worked example above — drawing modestly from an existing buffer can be entirely reasonable and may avoid a rate reduction altogether, provided the buffer is rebuilt afterward per the review-date discipline in Step 3. For a longer, sustained shift — a new baby's ongoing childcare cost, an eighteen-month career change — a buffer isn't the right tool, because the cost isn't temporary in the same sense; it's a genuine, ongoing change to the floor for the duration, and the rate itself needs to reflect that rather than being propped up by drawing down savings that were never meant to be a permanent income supplement.

A fourth worked example: relocation to a different cost-of-living area

A household relocating for a job opportunity — moving from a lower-cost region to a significantly higher-cost metro area, with a modest accompanying raise that doesn't fully offset the increased cost of living — experiences a transition that hits the floor side of the equation almost immediately and durably, rather than temporarily. Before the move, their take-home was $6,100 a month against a floor of $3,400, a gap of $2,700 (Bracket 3). After the move, take-home rises to $6,700, but the new region's floor — driven almost entirely by a much higher rent for a comparable home — comes to $5,300. The new gap is $1,400, a sharp drop into Bracket 2 despite the nominal raise.

This is a case where Step 3's review date needs a different character than the baby or home-purchase examples above, because a relocation to a genuinely higher-cost area isn't a temporary spike that resolves on its own after a few months —

the new floor is very likely the household's real floor going forward, not a transitional one. The review date here isn't about checking whether the floor has settled back down; it's about checking, six months in, whether the initial floor estimate for the new area was accurate once actual utility costs, insurance rates, and other regionally variable expenses are known with more certainty than they were during the pre-move planning stage. If the floor comes in lower than initially estimated once real bills arrive, the gap widens and the bracket-based rate can rise accordingly. If it comes in higher, the household needs an honest recalculation rather than continuing to apply a rate that was set against an overly optimistic pre-move estimate. Either way, this is a case where the transition itself doesn't end — the household has landed in a new, ongoing reality, and the review date exists to correct the initial estimate rather than to mark a return to a prior baseline that no longer applies.

A short exercise: mapping your own likely future transitions

Most of the transitions covered in this chapter are foreseeable well before they arrive — a planned pregnancy, a home purchase already being saved toward, a career change already under active consideration. Take a few minutes to list any transition you can reasonably foresee in the next two to three years, and for each one, make a rough estimate of how it would affect your floor (new recurring costs) or your gap (a temporary income change). You don't need precise numbers this far in advance — a reasonable range is enough. The value of this exercise isn't precision; it's removing the element of surprise from a transition's effect on your savings rate, so that when it arrives, you're recalculating a plan you'd already anticipated needing to adjust, rather than discovering for the first time, mid-transition, that your old rate no longer fits.

Distinguishing a transition from ordinary life-cost creep

It's worth drawing a clear line between the genuine transitions this chapter covers and the much more common, much less dramatic phenomenon of ordinary costs quietly rising over time — a rent increase at lease renewal, grocery prices drifting upward, an insurance premium that ticks up a little each year. These everyday cost increases are real and do affect the floor, but they don't call for this chapter's transition-reset framework; they call for the ordinary, periodic floor recalculation already built into Chapter 1's method and Chapter 9's annual review cycle. Treating every small cost increase as a "transition" that justifies pausing or resetting a savings rate risks turning a disciplined, occasional recalibration tool into a constant excuse to defer saving indefinitely, which undermines the entire purpose of building a rate around real numbers in the first place.

The practical distinguishing test: a genuine transition, of the kind this chapter addresses, involves either a discrete, identifiable event with a real start and (usually) a real end — a birth, a purchase, a job change — or a durable, one-time shift in the floor itself, like the relocation example above. Ordinary cost creep, by contrast, has no discrete event attached to it; it's the slow accumulation of small increases across an unchanged situation. A household experiencing ordinary cost creep should simply update their floor calculation at their next scheduled review and adjust their rate incrementally, the same routine maintenance any live financial plan requires — not treat every small increase as grounds for a formal transition-style reset, review date, and all.

A short exercise: sorting past cost changes into the two categories

Look back over the last two years of your own finances and list every meaningful cost change you can recall — a move, a new child, a job change, but also smaller things like a rent renewal or an insurance premium increase. Sort each one into "genuine transition" or "ordinary cost creep" using the distinguishing test above. For anything sorted as a genuine transition that you handled by simply forcing your old savings rate to hold anyway, note what that likely cost you — a missed adjustment, a quietly overdrawn buffer, a rate that got manually paused and never quite came back. This retrospective exercise tends to make the forward-looking version — mapping future transitions before they arrive — considerably more concrete, since it's grounded in real, specific things that already happened rather than abstract hypotheticals.

A note on transitions involving a partnership dissolution

A divorce or the dissolution of a long-term shared household is one of the more disruptive transitions this chapter's framework has to handle, because it typically hits both sides of the floor-and-gap equation simultaneously and in the same direction: income that was previously shared or coordinated splits into two separate households, while many fixed costs — housing chief among them — don't split cleanly in half, since two separate residences almost always cost more in combined total than the single shared residence they're replacing did. A household's floor after separation is very often not simply half of the prior shared floor; it's frequently close to, or even above, the full prior shared floor, now supported by only a fraction of the prior combined income.

This chapter's temporary floor reset applies directly, with one important adjustment to Step 3's review-date logic: unlike a new baby's childcare costs, which tend to follow a somewhat predictable trajectory as a child ages, or a home purchase's initial cost spike, which resolves within a few months by nature, a post-separation floor is often durable rather than temporary — closer to the relocation case covered earlier in this chapter than to the baby or home-purchase cases. The review date, in this specific transition, should function the way it did in the relocation example: a check on whether the new floor estimate was accurate, not an expectation that costs will settle back toward some prior shared baseline that no longer exists. A newly single household running this chapter's framework honestly, even if it produces a Bracket 1 rate for a period, is applying the exact same disciplined math this chapter argues for throughout — an honest number for a genuinely changed floor, rather than either an unsustainable rate held out of habit or an assumption that nothing needs to be recalculated at all.

A note on caring for an aging parent or family member

A transition that arrives with less advance planning time than most others covered in this chapter, and that's becoming more common as a real financial event across a working life: taking on a caregiving role for an aging parent or family member, whether that means direct financial support, absorbing a new household member's living costs, or reducing paid working hours to provide care directly. Each of these variants hits the floor-and-gap equation differently, and the distinction matters rather than treating "caregiving" as a single undifferentiated transition.

Direct financial support — regularly covering a portion of another person's costs — adds a new, real line item to the floor, calculated the same way any other new recurring cost would be under Step 1's recalculation. A family member moving into the household changes the floor's underlying cost structure directly — more groceries, potentially a larger housing cost, additional utilities — again, a straightforward floor recalculation once the new numbers are known. Reducing paid working hours to provide direct care, by contrast, hits the income side of the gap rather than the floor, mechanically identical to the career-change worked example earlier in this chapter, just triggered by a caregiving obligation rather than a chosen career shift.

What distinguishes this transition from most others in this chapter is its frequently uncertain duration and trajectory — unlike a baby's childcare costs, which tend to decline over a knowable number of years, or a home purchase's cost spike, which resolves within months, a caregiving obligation's timeline and intensity can be genuinely unpredictable, sometimes stable for years, sometimes escalating without much warning. This uncertainty argues for a shorter review cycle than this chapter's other examples — a quarterly check rather than a single fixed review date months out — specifically because the floor itself may need to be recalculated more than once as the situation evolves, rather than assumed stable for a full standard review period once the initial transition-floor calculation is done.

This transition also interacts directly with Chapter 7's goal-timeline ladder in a way worth flagging: a household anticipating a caregiving obligation on the horizon, even one without a firm start date, has good reason to treat it as a near-term contingency when deciding how much of their gap belongs in accessible savings versus tax-advantaged accounts, rather than waiting until the obligation actually arrives to make that adjustment. Building a modest, explicitly named accessible reserve ahead of an anticipated caregiving need — distinct from the general emergency buffer, and distinct from any other named goal — gives a household real flexibility to absorb the first several months of a new caregiving floor without needing to immediately force a full transition-reset calculation the moment the obligation begins.

Chapter 5 — The Catch-Up Math for Late Starters

The situation

Someone turning 45 realizes, doing the arithmetic for the first time in any real detail, that they have a fraction of what a standard age-based benchmark suggests they should have saved by now. The instinct that follows is often either paralysis — treating the gap as unrecoverable and giving up on any structured plan — or a vague resolution to "save more" without any specific number attached to it, which tends to produce the same disappointing result as no plan at all. Neither reaction is grounded in the actual math, which is calculable, specific, and considerably more encouraging than the paralysis suggests, though it does require a materially different rate than someone who started twenty years earlier.

The mechanics

Compound growth is not linear, and the practical consequence of that fact is the entire reason a late start requires a disproportionately larger monthly contribution to reach the same eventual target — not just a proportionally larger one.

Money invested earlier has more compounding periods ahead of it, and each additional year of compounding adds more in absolute terms than the year before it, because growth is happening on an ever-larger base. A dollar invested at 25 has roughly twice as many years to compound as a dollar invested at 45, assuming a target retirement age in the mid-to-late sixties, and the difference in eventual value isn't double — depending on assumed returns, it's frequently three to four times as much, because the additional early years are compounding on top of each other rather than simply adding up.

This is worth making concrete with a standard compound growth calculation, using a illustrative long-run average annual return commonly cited for a diversified portfolio over long periods — this book uses 7% throughout this chapter as a round, widely used planning assumption, not a guarantee, and actual returns in any specific period will vary, sometimes substantially, from any long-run average. Using this assumption: a single dollar invested at age 25 and left untouched until age 65 — forty years of compounding — grows to roughly $14.97. The same dollar invested at age 45 and left until age 65 — twenty years of compounding — grows to roughly \$3.87. Half the time doesn't produce half the growth. It produces about a quarter of it, because compounding is exponential, not linear, and the earliest years contribute disproportionately to the final total precisely because everything that follows compounds on top of them.

The practical consequence for a late starter is that reaching the same eventual target requires a monthly contribution rate that rises faster than the simple ratio of years remaining would suggest. Someone starting twenty years later than a hypothetical early starter doesn't need to save twice as much per month to catch up to the same target by the same age — the shortfall in compounding time means they typically need three to four times the monthly contribution, not two, because the missing years were disproportionately valuable ones.

The framework: the catch-up multiplier

Step 1 — Establish your actual target, in today's dollars, using a realistic retirement-income need rather than an arbitrary round number. Chapter 8 covers how to calculate this target properly using established replacement-ratio research;

for this chapter's purposes, use whatever target figure applies to your own situation, worked out using that chapter's method or a comparable calculation you trust.

Step 2 — Calculate the monthly contribution required to reach that target from your current starting point, using your actual number of years until your planned retirement age and a conservative assumed return. This is a standard future-value-of-an-annuity calculation, widely available through free, reputable retirement calculators from major financial institutions and through straightforward compound-interest formulas — this book won't reproduce the full formula here, since the arithmetic itself is mechanical and the calculators are genuinely reliable; what this chapter provides is the framework for interpreting the result honestly.

Step 3 — Compare the required monthly contribution against your current bracket-based rate from Chapter 2, and treat the gap between them as real information, not a verdict. If the required contribution meaningfully exceeds what your current gap can sustainably support, per Chapter 1's floor test, you have three honest levers, and only three: increase the gap (raise income, reduce the floor), extend the timeline (a later planned retirement age, even by a few years, meaningfully reduces the required monthly figure because it restores some of the lost compounding time), or adjust the target itself (a more modest, still-dignified retirement income need lowers the required contribution proportionally). Pretending a fourth lever exists — hoping for unusually high returns to close the gap without changing any of the three real inputs — isn't a plan; it's a bet, and this book doesn't recommend building a retirement plan around an assumption of above-average luck.

Step 4 — Use the catch-up contribution provisions available through most tax-advantaged retirement accounts once eligible. Many retirement account structures allow additional contribution amounts beyond the standard annual limit starting at a specific age, a real and verifiable feature of the U.S. retirement system worth using fully once eligible — check current limits and eligibility ages directly with your plan administrator or a tax professional, since specific dollar figures and thresholds are adjusted periodically and this book deliberately doesn't cite a number likely to be outdated by the time you're reading it.

Worked example

Someone starting at age 45, planning to retire at 65 (twenty years of compounding), with a target that requires an eventual portfolio of $850,000 in today's dollars, and $60,000 already saved, needs to calculate the monthly contribution required to close the remaining gap over twenty years at a 7% assumed return. Working through the standard future-value calculation: the existing $60,000 grows to roughly $232,000 over twenty years untouched. The remaining gap to the $850,000 target is $618,000, which at a 7% assumed annual return requires a monthly contribution of roughly $1,190 sustained for the full twenty years.

Compare this to what an early starter would have needed for the identical target. Someone starting at 25 with forty years of compounding and no existing balance needs a monthly contribution of roughly $410 to reach the same $850,000 target — less than a third of the late starter's required figure, despite the late starter needing to close a gap that's smaller in absolute dollar terms once their existing $60,000 head start is factored in. This is the catch-up multiplier in concrete form: half the working years doesn't require double the contribution. It requires roughly three times it, because the lost compounding years were the most valuable ones the early starter had.

If $1,190 a month exceeds what the person's current bracket-based rate can sustainably support, Step 3's three levers apply directly. Extending the planned retirement age from 65 to 68 — three additional years of compounding on both the existing balance and future contributions — reduces the required monthly contribution meaningfully, often by 20% or more depending on the specific numbers, because those three years are working on an already-larger base than the earliest years would have been. A modest reduction in the target itself, say to $720,000 by accepting a somewhat leaner but still genuinely comfortable retirement income, has a similar effect. Neither lever is a failure to plan for retirement properly — both are honest, calculable adjustments to a plan that has to work with the years actually available, not the years a person wishes they'd started with.

A second worked example: starting even later

Someone starting at 55, planning to retire at 67 (twelve years of compounding), with $40,000 already saved and the same $850,000 target, faces an even steeper multiplier. The existing balance grows to roughly $90,000 over twelve years. The remaining gap of $760,000, closed over twelve years at 7%, requires a monthly contribution of roughly $3,600 — a figure that, for most households at most income levels, simply won't fit inside even a Bracket 4 gap without real strain.

This is exactly the situation where Step 3's three levers stop being optional refinements and become the actual plan. Extending the retirement age from 67 to 70 adds three more years of compounding, which, combined with continued Social Security accrual during those years (a real, separate factor beyond the scope of this chapter's calculation but genuinely relevant to a full retirement-income picture), can reduce the required monthly figure substantially — often by 25 to 35% in a case this compressed, since additional years matter disproportionately more when the base is already smaller and the timeline is already short. Combined with a modest downward adjustment to the target and maximizing available catch-up contribution provisions from Step 4, a genuinely workable plan emerges from what looked, at first glance, like an impossible number — not by ignoring the math, but by adjusting the actual inputs the math depends on, deliberately and specifically, rather than hoping the number becomes achievable through wishful thinking alone.

Why paralysis is the wrong response to this math

A late start, however steep the required contribution looks on paper, is never a reason to abandon a structured plan in favor of doing nothing, and it helps to be direct about why. Every month spent not contributing at all, while waiting to feel more prepared or more able to hit an ideal number, is a month of lost compounding that makes the eventual required rate even higher than the calculation above shows — the math in this chapter only gets worse with additional delay, never better. A late starter contributing an imperfect but real amount today, even one below the fully calculated catch-up figure, is meaningfully better positioned than the same person waiting another two or three years to start once the "right" number feels achievable. The catch-up math in this chapter is a planning tool for setting an informed target, not a threshold that has to be fully met before it's worth starting at all.

Common objections and how to handle them

"What if I can't realistically hit the calculated monthly figure at all, even after adjusting the levers?" Contribute the maximum your current bracket-based gap can sustainably support, and treat the shortfall honestly as information for the levers in Step 3 rather than a reason to disengage from the plan entirely. A retirement funded partially by savings and partially by a longer working life or a more modest target isn't a failure — it's a real, honest plan built from real numbers, which is a meaningfully better position than an unexamined hope that things will somehow work out.

"Is a 7% assumed return too optimistic, or too conservative?" This book deliberately uses a widely cited, moderate planning assumption rather than either an optimistic or pessimistic outlier, and readers should feel free to run the same calculation at a more conservative assumption (5 to 6%) to see how sensitive their own required contribution is to that assumption — a plan that only works at an optimistic return assumption is worth stress-testing against a more conservative one before treating it as reliable.

A note on Social Security and the catch-up calculation

This chapter's worked examples calculate a required monthly contribution against a full retirement-income target, without netting out any expected Social Security benefit — a deliberate simplification, and worth explaining rather than leaving implicit. Social Security is a real, meaningful component of most retirement plans in the United States, and for a late starter specifically, it functions as a partial floor beneath the catch-up calculation: a benefit that continues regardless of how the personal-savings side of the plan performs, which somewhat softens the real-world stakes of the catch-up math compared to what the raw numbers in this chapter suggest on their own.

The reason this chapter's calculations don't build Social Security in directly is that an accurate estimate depends on a specific, individual earnings record and claiming-age decision that no general worked example can approximate responsibly — a late starter's own benefit estimate, available directly through the Social Security Administration's own tools using their actual earnings history, is a far more accurate input than any generic assumption this book could offer. A practical way to fold it into this chapter's framework: obtain your own estimated benefit at your planned claiming age, convert it to an equivalent portfolio value using the same sustainable-withdrawal-rate logic covered in Chapter 8, and subtract that from your Step 1 target before running the required-contribution calculation in Step 2. For most late starters, this meaningfully reduces the required monthly figure — sometimes substantially — without changing anything about the underlying catch-up multiplier mechanic this chapter is built around.

A short exercise: running your own catch-up number

Using your current age, planned retirement age, existing retirement savings balance, and a target from Chapter 8's replacement-ratio method (or a placeholder figure if you haven't run that chapter's calculation yet), use any reputable, free retirement calculator to solve for the monthly contribution required to close the gap between your existing balance's projected future value and your target. Compare that required figure against your current bracket-based rate from Chapter 2. If the two are close, your current trajectory is likely on track without further adjustment. If the required figure is meaningfully higher, revisit Step 3's three levers — timeline, target, and contribution — one at a time, and note how much each one alone moves the required monthly figure. Seeing the actual sensitivity of each lever, rather than guessing at it, is usually what turns a catch-up calculation from a source of anxiety into an actual, workable plan.

A note on catching up while also carrying Chapter 3's high-interest debt

A late starter who's also carrying high-interest debt faces a genuine tension between two chapters' recommendations, and it's worth resolving directly rather than leaving the reader to guess which framework takes priority. Chapter 3's rate-threshold split argues for weighting the large majority of a household's gap toward high-interest payoff before general saving. This chapter's catch-up math argues for a large, sustained contribution toward retirement to close a compressed timeline. Both are correct on their own terms, and the resolution isn't to average them into a mediocre compromise on both fronts — it's to run them in the correct sequence.

Chapter 3's math still wins first: a guaranteed double-digit return from clearing high-interest debt outperforms the uncertain return being chased by an aggressive retirement contribution, even for a late starter with a compressed timeline, because a dollar directed at 22% APR debt is doing more for the household's total financial position than that same dollar could do invested at an assumed 7%. The correct sequence for a late starter carrying high-interest debt is: capture the employer match (Step 1 in both chapters' frameworks agree on this), then apply Chapter 3's aggressive debt-payoff split until the high-interest debt clears, then run this chapter's catch-up calculation against the now-larger gap that debt payoff has freed up. The catch-up timeline effectively starts the day the debt clears, not the day this chapter's math was first run — which means being honest, in the Step 3 lever discussion, that debt payoff itself is often eating into the years available for the catch-up contribution to work, and the three levers (timeline, target, contribution) may need to lean more heavily on an extended retirement age than they would for an equivalent late starter without debt in the picture.

A note on employer-match vesting schedules and the catch-up calculation

Some employer retirement plans attach a vesting schedule to matched contributions — meaning the employer's matching dollars don't become fully, permanently the employee's own until a specified period of continuous employment has passed, even though the employee's own contributions are always fully theirs immediately. This matters specifically for the catch-up calculations in this chapter because a late starter changing jobs, which is common enough at the exact ages this chapter's worked examples focus on, can lose unvested matched dollars entirely if they leave before the vesting period completes — a real, if often overlooked, risk to factor into any catch-up plan that assumes a full employer match as a fixed input.

The practical adjustment: when running Step 2's required-contribution calculation, a late starter who anticipates a job change within a plan's vesting period should run the calculation twice — once assuming the full employer match survives, and once assuming only the vested portion does — and treat the more conservative of the two figures as the number to actually plan around, rather than assuming the more favorable scenario by default. This isn't a reason to avoid a job change that might otherwise make good career sense; it's simply a reason to build the catch-up plan around a number that holds regardless of which scenario actually unfolds, checking the plan's specific vesting schedule directly with the employer's plan documentation rather than assuming a standard timeline that may not match the specific plan in question.

A note on the emotional weight of the catch-up multiplier, and why the arithmetic still comes first

Seeing the actual multiplier from this chapter's worked examples — a required contribution three or four times larger than an equivalent early starter's, for half the working years — can land harder than most of the arithmetic elsewhere in this book, because it's not just a calculation, it's often the first time the real cost of a delayed start has been made fully concrete rather than left as a vague, background worry. That reaction deserves a direct response rather than being moved past purely mechanically, because a late starter who closes this chapter feeling defeated rather than equipped has, in a real sense, gotten the opposite of what the arithmetic was meant to provide.

The multiplier is large because compounding is genuinely, mathematically powerful — which is exactly why the required contribution to catch up is also so much larger, not because catching up is somehow uniquely difficult or unfair in a way other financial challenges aren't. The same compounding math that makes an early start so valuable is the same math a late starter can still put to work for every year that remains, starting now, at whatever rate is actually achievable. A late starter contributing a real, calculated amount for the next twenty years is still capturing two decades of the exact compounding effect that makes this whole chapter's arithmetic work in the first place — a meaningfully better outcome than either an unexamined smaller contribution made without a plan, or no contribution at all made while waiting for a level of readiness that delay itself makes progressively harder to reach.

Chapter 6 — Savings Rate for Variable and Freelance Income

The situation

A freelance consultant earns $9,200 one month, $3,100 the next, and $6,800 the month after that — real numbers from a real three-month stretch, not an unusual outlier for someone whose income depends on project timing and client cycles rather than a fixed salary. Every piece of savings-rate advice this person has encountered assumes a stable monthly figure to apply a percentage to, and none of it tells them what to actually do with a month that brings in a third of the prior one, or how to avoid either overcommitting during a strong month or abandoning savings entirely during a weak one.

The mechanics

A savings rate calculated against a single month's income, applied literally to variable earnings, produces exactly the instability this person is experiencing: a large transfer during a strong month that may not have accounted for an upcoming weak one, followed by a skipped or reduced transfer during the weak month that undermines confidence in the whole system.

This isn't a discipline problem — it's the wrong denominator problem from Chapter 1, applied to time instead of just to the floor. Just as a flat percentage of income ignores the fixed-cost floor beneath it, a savings rate calculated against a single month's income ignores the fact that variable income only makes sense evaluated across a longer window, not a single arbitrary thirty-day slice of it.

There's a second mechanical wrinkle specific to variable and self-employment income that a salaried savings-rate calculation doesn't need to handle: self-employment tax and quarterly estimated tax obligations sit on top of ordinary living costs in a way that a salaried worker's withheld paycheck already handles invisibly. Treating gross freelance income as if it were equivalent to a salaried worker's take-home pay overstates the actual gap available for the floor-test math from Chapter 1, because a real tax obligation hasn't yet been carved out of it the way withholding automatically carves it out of a salaried paycheck.

The framework: the trailing-average rate

Step 1 — Set aside tax obligations first, before any floor or gap calculation. For most self-employed income, a reasonable starting estimate is 25 to 30% of gross income set aside for federal and state tax obligations, adjusted to your actual bracket and location with a tax professional's input — this is not optional and not part of the savings rate; it's a pre-tax, pre-floor deduction that has to happen before the rest of this chapter's math is meaningful. Route this into a dedicated tax-holding account, separate from both spending and savings, immediately upon receiving each payment.

Step 2 — Calculate a trailing twelve-month average of post-tax income, updated monthly, rather than reacting to any single month. This smooths the genuine volatility of variable income into a number stable enough to apply the fixed-cost floor test and bracket math from Chapters 1 and 2 meaningfully. A single strong or weak month doesn't move a twelve-month trailing average nearly as much as it moves the raw monthly figure, which is precisely the point — the average approximates the stable, ongoing income level the rest of this book's math is designed to work against.

Step 3 — Set your savings rate against the trailing average, not the current month's actual income, and let it stay fixed as a dollar amount for a full month regardless of what that specific month brings in. In a strong month, the excess above the trailing average doesn't automatically become extra savings — it becomes a contribution to an income-smoothing buffer, covered in Step 4, which is what actually makes a stable rate possible against unstable income. In a weak month, the fixed transfer still executes as planned, drawing if necessary from the smoothing buffer rather than being skipped outright.

Step 4 — Build and maintain an income-smoothing buffer, separate from an emergency buffer, sized to roughly one to two months of your trailing-average post-tax income. This buffer's specific job is to absorb the gap between what a weak month actually brings in and what the fixed savings-rate transfer requires, refilled automatically during stronger-than-average months. This is a genuinely different tool from the emergency buffer covered in this library's companion volume on automation — an emergency buffer exists for the rare true crisis; an income-smoothing buffer exists for the routine, expected variability that comes with the territory of variable income and gets used and refilled constantly as a normal part of how the system runs.

Worked example

The freelance consultant from this chapter's opening has a trailing twelve-month gross income average of $6,800 a month. After setting aside 28% for taxes, their trailing post-tax average is $4,896. Their fixed-cost floor, calculated using Chapter 1's method, is $3,400, leaving a trailing average gap of $1,496 — placing them in Bracket 2 from Chapter 2's framework, with a sustainable rate around 30% of the gap: roughly $449 a month.

In the $9,200 month referenced at the opening, after the 28% tax set-aside ($2,576), post-tax income is $6,624 — well above the trailing average. The $449 savings transfer still fires as planned, and the surplus above what the trailing-average floor-and-gap math accounts for ($6,624 minus $3,400 floor minus $449 savings, leaving $2,775 of unplanned excess) is split: a portion tops off the income-smoothing buffer if it's below its one-to-two-month target, and the remainder becomes genuinely discretionary or an opportunistic extra contribution, at the household's discretion, rather than an automatic obligation.

In the $3,100 month, after tax set-aside ($868), post-tax income is $2,232 — below the fixed-cost floor of $3,400 even before touching the savings transfer. The $449 savings transfer still fires as planned, but the floor itself is covered partly by income and partly by a $1,168 draw from the income-smoothing buffer, which exists precisely for a month like this one. Nothing about the household's savings plan breaks or requires manual intervention — the buffer absorbed the shortfall exactly as designed, and the trailing average, recalculated at month's end, shifts only slightly, since one weak month among twelve doesn't move a twelve-month average dramatically.

A second worked example: a seasonal business

A small business owner with genuinely seasonal income — strong revenue for five months a year, minimal revenue for the remaining seven — faces an even more extreme version of this chapter's core problem, and the trailing-average approach handles it the same way, just with a larger buffer requirement. Rather than the one-to-two-month buffer sufficient for the freelance consultant's moderate month-to-month variability, a genuinely seasonal income pattern typically requires a smoothing buffer closer to four to six months of trailing-average expenses, sized specifically against the length of the low season rather than a generic rule of thumb. During the five strong months, a larger share of income beyond the fixed transfer goes toward building this seasonal buffer specifically, rather than toward general discretionary spending or additional investment, precisely because the seven lean months ahead are a known, predictable draw on it rather than a rare emergency. This is a case where the smoothing buffer isn't a backstop for occasional bad luck — it's a core, load-bearing part of the annual plan, sized deliberately against a known seasonal pattern rather than an unpredictable one.

Common objections and how to handle them

"What if my income is trending meaningfully up or down, not just varying around a stable average?" A pure twelve-month trailing average can lag a genuine trend, whether growth or decline, and it's worth supplementing it with a periodic gut-check: if the most recent three to four months are consistently and meaningfully above or below the full trailing average, that's a signal the average itself may need a deliberate manual adjustment rather than waiting for twelve months of data to fully catch up. A business genuinely growing shouldn't be stuck calculating its savings rate against a stale, understated average indefinitely — recalibrate manually when a real trend is evident, then let the trailing average resume tracking normally from the new baseline.

"Isn't setting aside 25 to 30% for taxes overly conservative in some cases, or not enough in others?" The exact figure depends heavily on total income, deductions, state of residence, and business structure, and this chapter's range is a reasonable starting estimate, not a substitute for an actual tax professional's calculation specific to your situation — get a real number from a professional as soon as your variable income becomes a meaningful, ongoing part of your household finances, and adjust the set-aside percentage to match rather than relying on a rough rule of thumb indefinitely.

"Should the smoothing buffer live in the same account as my emergency buffer?" Keep them separate, even though both are, in a sense, money held in reserve. An emergency buffer is meant to be touched rarely, for genuine crises, and refilled slowly after a real event. An income-smoothing buffer is meant to be touched routinely, as a normal and expected part of how variable income gets managed month to month, and refilled constantly during strong months. Blending the two into a single account risks either a smoothing draw quietly eroding true emergency protection, or an overly conservative reluctance to use the smoothing buffer the way it's actually meant to be used, out of a mistaken sense that it should be preserved the same way an emergency fund would be.

A note on irregular large payments

Variable income sometimes arrives not as ordinary month-to-month fluctuation but as an occasional large, lumpy payment — a book advance, an annual bonus, a single large contract that dwarfs a typical month's earnings. This is a distinct case from the routine variability this chapter's trailing-average method is built to smooth, and it deserves its own explicit rule rather than being folded into the twelve-month average, where a single unusually large month can distort the average for most of a year afterward.

The practical fix: exclude genuinely one-off, irregular large payments from the trailing-average calculation entirely, and instead apply this book's bracket math (Chapter 2) directly to that specific lump sum, treating it as its own isolated calculation rather than smoothing it into ordinary monthly income. Calculate a floor-and-gap ratio for the lump sum itself against any specific costs it's earmarked to cover, and apply a bracket-appropriate percentage of the remainder to savings, exactly as Chapter 2 describes for ordinary income — just applied once, to the lump sum, rather than monthly. This keeps the trailing average clean and representative of genuinely ordinary income variability, while still ensuring a large one-off payment gets a deliberate, calculated savings treatment rather than either disappearing into lifestyle spending untouched or distorting a full year of otherwise-accurate trailing-average math.

A short exercise: building your own trailing average

If you have at least six months of income history available, calculate a trailing average now, even if it's not yet a full twelve months — a six-month average is meaningfully more stable than reacting to any single month, even though it's not as smooth as the full twelve-month version this chapter recommends once enough history exists. Subtract your estimated tax set-aside percentage, then apply Chapter 1's floor test and Chapter 2's bracket math to the result exactly as this chapter's worked examples do. If you don't yet have six months of income history — a freelance practice or business still in its first several months — use your best honest estimate of a sustainable ongoing average based on the work already booked or reasonably expected, treat that number as provisional, and recalculate properly once real history accumulates. A provisional number, revisited monthly as real data arrives, is considerably more useful than waiting a full year to apply any structure to a variable income at all.

A note on transitioning from salaried to variable income

A specific version of this chapter's problem deserves its own mention: someone leaving a stable salaried role to become self-employed doesn't have a twelve-month trailing average to build from at all in the early months — there's no history yet, only a projection, and projections for a new self-employed venture are notoriously optimistic in the first year. The practical fix during this specific window is to treat the transition using Chapter 4's framework first, recalculating the floor and gap against a deliberately conservative income estimate — often meaningfully below whatever the optimistic business plan projects — for the first six to twelve months, rather than assuming the trailing-average method from this chapter can be applied before any real trailing data exists to average.

Once six months of real, actual income history accumulates, shift over to this chapter's trailing-average method as described, using the real figures rather than the original projection, even if the real figures come in below what was originally hoped for. This staged approach — Chapter 4's conservative transition floor first, this chapter's trailing-average method once real data exists — avoids the common and costly mistake of setting a savings rate against an optimistic first-year revenue projection that a new business, however promising, frequently doesn't hit in its first several months of real operation.

A second short exercise: stress-testing your buffer against your worst real month

Look back through your actual income history for the single worst month on record — not a hypothetical worst case, but the actual lowest month that's already happened. Confirm that your current income-smoothing buffer, sized per this chapter's one-to-two-month (or four-to-six-month for genuinely seasonal income) guidance, would have fully covered the gap between that worst real month and your fixed-cost floor, with the fixed savings transfer still firing as planned. If it wouldn't have, the buffer is undersized relative to the volatility you've actually experienced, regardless of what a generic sizing rule suggests — increase it until a repeat of your actual worst month, not just a theoretical one, is something the system can absorb without manual intervention.

A note on hybrid income — a base salary plus variable commission or bonus

A meaningful number of workers earn a genuinely hybrid income: a stable, predictable base salary combined with a variable commission, bonus, or overtime component that can swing significantly from one pay period to the next. This is neither the purely stable salaried case nor the purely variable freelance case this chapter otherwise addresses, and it's worth showing how the two halves of this book's framework combine for it rather than forcing a hybrid earner to choose one method and ignore the other.

The correct approach: treat the stable base salary using the standard, non-averaged floor-and-gap method from Chapters 1 and 2, since that portion of income is genuinely predictable and doesn't need smoothing. Treat only the variable component — commission, bonus, overtime — using this chapter's trailing-average method, calculating a separate trailing average for that portion alone rather than blending it into the stable base. The two pieces then combine: a bracket-based rate calculated against the stable base's own gap, plus an additional contribution calculated against the trailing-average variable component's own gap, using Chapter 2's bracket math applied separately to each. This split-treatment approach avoids two common mistakes in either direction — treating the entire hybrid income as fully stable, which risks a savings rate that assumes a bonus which doesn't always materialize at the same level, and treating the entire income as fully variable, which unnecessarily smooths a base salary that was never actually unpredictable in the first place and doesn't need a trailing average to be trusted.

A worked example: the split-treatment method applied

A sales representative earns a $3,800 monthly base salary, entirely predictable, plus commission that has ranged from $900 to $4,200 a month over the past eighteen months with no clear seasonal pattern — genuinely variable rather than hybrid-seasonal. Their fixed-cost floor is $3,200. Applying the split-treatment method: the base salary alone produces a gap of $600 against the floor ($3,800 minus $3,200), a thin Bracket 1 gap, with a sustainable rate around 18% of that gap — roughly $108 a month, calculated using the standard, non-averaged method since the base salary needs no smoothing.

The commission component, averaged over the trailing twelve months at roughly $2,100 a month, is treated as its own separate income stream with no fixed costs of its own to subtract, since the floor was already fully covered by the base salary calculation above — commission income above a covered floor is, in effect, entirely gap, placing it toward the upper end of this book's bracket range. Applying a rate around 55% of this second gap produces roughly $1,155 a month from the commission stream. The combined monthly savings rate — $108 from the stable base plus $1,155 from the trailing-average commission — comes to $1,263, moved as two separate automatic transfers on two different schedules: the base-salary portion moving on the same day the salary lands, predictable and steady, and the commission portion recalculated and transferred monthly against the updated trailing average, exactly as this chapter's core method describes for a purely variable earner.

Notice what this split accomplishes that either a fully-stable or fully-variable treatment would have missed. Treating the whole $5,900 average monthly income as stable and applying a single bracket calculation against it would have overstated how reliable that full figure actually is, since roughly a third of it (in a weak commission month) or nearly three-quarters of it (in a strong one) is genuinely unpredictable. Treating the whole income as variable and trailing-averaging all of it together would have unnecessarily smoothed the $3,800 base, which never needed smoothing in the first place since it arrives at the same reliable figure every single month regardless of performance. The split-treatment method captures both truths at once, applying the right kind of math to each portion of the income separately rather than forcing one method to do a job it wasn't built for.

A note on when the split-treatment method isn't worth the added complexity

The split-treatment method above adds real precision, but it also adds real bookkeeping — two separate trailing calculations, two separate transfers, two separate schedules to maintain. For a hybrid earner whose variable component is genuinely small relative to their stable base — commission or bonus income that rarely exceeds 10 to 15% of total pay — the added precision often isn't worth the added complexity, and a simpler approach serves nearly as well: treat the full income as stable using the base salary's own predictable figure, and treat any variable component received in a given month as a one-off lump sum per this chapter's earlier guidance on irregular large payments, applying Chapter 2's bracket math to it directly, once, rather than building out an ongoing trailing-average system for a income stream that's a minor part of the overall picture.

The threshold worth applying here: if the variable component regularly makes up more than roughly 20% of total income, or if its absence in a weak month would meaningfully affect whether the fixed-cost floor gets covered, the full split-treatment method earns its added complexity. Below that threshold, the simpler lump-sum treatment captures nearly all of the same accuracy with a fraction of the ongoing maintenance, and a savings-rate system that's simple enough to actually maintain consistently over years beats a more precise one that's abandoned within a few months because it asked for more upkeep than the marginal accuracy was worth.

Chapter 7 — Retirement Accounts vs. Accessible Savings

The situation

A household earning $7,600 a month take-home, with a well-calculated gap and a sustainable Bracket 3 savings rate of $2,200 a month, has correctly determined *how much* to save. What they haven't determined is *where* it should go — how much into tax-advantaged retirement accounts that penalize early withdrawal, and how much into accessible savings they can actually reach before retirement age, given a genuine, near-term goal of buying a home in roughly four years. Every dollar routed the wrong way either forfeits real tax advantage or gets locked up somewhere it's needed too soon to reach without penalty.

The mechanics

This is a distinct question from the account-architecture mechanics covered in this library's companion volume, which focuses on *how* to automate transfers into whichever accounts a household has already decided to fund. This chapter answers the question that has to come first: what proportion of a given savings rate should be split between retirement-specific, tax-advantaged accounts and general accessible savings, given that the two serve genuinely different jobs and carry genuinely different tradeoffs.

Tax-advantaged retirement accounts offer real, quantifiable benefits — reduced current taxable income, tax-deferred or tax-free growth depending on account type, and in many cases an employer match that functions as an immediate, guaranteed return well beyond what any accessible savings vehicle can offer. Against those benefits sits a real cost: money in most retirement-specific accounts generally can't be accessed before a specified age without a meaningful penalty, on top of any taxes owed. That penalty is a real, structural feature, not an inconvenience to plan around casually — it exists specifically to discourage early withdrawal, and it does its job effectively enough that treating retirement-account money as available for anything short of a genuine emergency, or a goal genuinely decades away, is planning against the account's actual purpose.

Accessible savings — a standard brokerage account, high-yield savings, or similar vehicles without the early-withdrawal restriction — offer none of the tax-advantaged growth benefit but full liquidity: the money is there when a goal arrives, whether that goal is five years away or fifteen, without needing to pay a penalty to reach it. The right split between the two isn't a matter of picking one as universally superior; it's a matter of matching each dollar of savings to the actual timeline of the goal it's meant to serve.

The framework: the goal-timeline ladder

Step 1 — Always capture a full employer retirement match first, before any other allocation decision. This step repeats from Chapter 3 deliberately, because it's close to a universal rule regardless of what else is going on in a household's savings plan: an employer match is an immediate, guaranteed return that essentially no other allocation choice can beat, and skipping it to prioritize accessible savings for a near-term goal is very rarely the correct trade once the actual numbers are run.

Step 2 — Sort every active savings goal by timeline, not by size or emotional priority. A goal genuinely 20-plus years away (standard retirement) belongs almost entirely in tax-advantaged retirement accounts, since the early-withdrawal restriction is irrelevant to a goal that far out, and the tax advantage compounds meaningfully over that many years. A goal five years or fewer away (a home down payment, a wedding, a planned sabbatical) belongs almost entirely in accessible savings, since a retirement account's early-withdrawal penalty would erode a meaningful chunk of a goal on that timeline if the money had to be pulled out early to fund it. A goal in the middle distance — seven to fifteen years out — is the genuinely judgment-dependent case, and Step 3 addresses it directly.

Step 3 — For a middle-distance goal, weigh the specific certainty of the timeline against the tax advantage being forfeited. A goal with a firm, largely fixed date (a planned home purchase already scoped and priced) should lean toward accessible savings even at ten or more years out, since the certainty of needing the full amount on a specific date outweighs the tax benefit of a vehicle that might not be reachable without penalty by then. A goal with genuine flexibility in its timing (an aspirational early retirement that could slip a few years without real consequence) can lean further toward tax-advantaged accounts, since some flexibility exists to delay access if needed, and certain retirement-account structures do offer penalty-free access mechanisms starting at specific ages below standard retirement age, worth researching with a tax professional for a household seriously planning around this middle-distance case.

Step 4 — Beyond any specific named goal, direct remaining long-horizon savings — money with no fixed near-term purpose — toward maximizing available tax-advantaged space before defaulting to a general accessible account. Once every near- and middle-distance goal has an allocation, money left in the gap with no specific timeline attached is, by default, serving the same job as standard retirement savings: growth over a genuinely long horizon, which is exactly what tax-advantaged accounts are structurally built to reward.

Worked example

The household from this chapter's opening has a $2,200 monthly gap-based savings rate, a $9,400/year employer retirement match cap (fully captured by a specific contribution percentage), and two active goals: standard retirement (30-plus years out) and a home down payment (4 years out, firm target of $62,000, $14,000 already saved in accessible savings).

Applying the ladder: Step 1 captures the full employer match first — the contribution required to get it comes off the top of the $2,200, say $650 a month, into a tax-advantaged account. Step 2 sorts the two goals: retirement is a clear long-horizon case, and the home purchase, with a firm four-year target, is a clear near-term case that belongs in accessible savings despite forfeiting any tax advantage on that portion. Working backward from the $48,000 remaining down-payment target over 48 months requires roughly $1,000 a month into accessible savings. The remaining $550 of the $2,200 gap, with no specific near-term goal attached, follows Step 4 into additional tax-advantaged retirement contributions beyond the matched amount, assuming the household has room remaining within their account's contribution limits for the year.

The resulting split — $1,200 a month ($650 plus $550) into tax-advantaged retirement accounts, $1,000 a month into accessible savings — reflects the actual timeline of each dollar's job, not an arbitrary even split or a default toward whichever account type feels more virtuous. Reversing the split, over-funding accessible savings at the expense of the employer match or long-horizon retirement contributions, would forfeit real, calculable value; over-funding retirement accounts at the expense of the firm four-year home goal would risk needing to access retirement funds early, incurring a real penalty, when the down-payment date arrives.

A second worked example: the middle-distance case

A household with a well-funded retirement trajectory and no immediate five-year goal is weighing an aspirational goal of stepping back from full-time work at 55, roughly twelve years out from their current age — a genuine middle-distance case per Step 3. Because the goal has real flexibility in its exact timing (a delay to 57 or 58 wouldn't meaningfully undermine the plan) and because certain tax-advantaged account structures offer penalty-free access mechanisms starting at ages below the standard threshold, worth confirming with a tax professional for their specific account types, the household leans this allocation more heavily toward tax-advantaged accounts than a firm, inflexible twelve-year goal would warrant — roughly 70% tax-advantaged, 30% accessible, rather than the closer-to-even split a firm middle-distance goal might call for. This is a deliberate, informed tradeoff, made explicitly rather than defaulted into, and it's the kind of judgment call this chapter's framework is built to surface clearly rather than leave to guesswork.

Common objections and how to handle them

"What if I have multiple near-term goals competing for the same accessible-savings allocation?" Rank them explicitly by both timeline and importance, and fund them in that order rather than splitting evenly across all of them by default — a goal with a firmer date and higher priority should be fully funded before a softer, lower-priority goal gets any allocation at all, since an even split across competing goals risks under-funding the one that actually has a hard deadline.

"Isn't it safer to just keep everything accessible, in case I need it?" This forfeits real, calculable tax advantage and, for any portion of an employer match left uncaptured, forfeits guaranteed free money as well — a cost that's easy to underweight because it's invisible in the moment (nothing looks wrong with an all-accessible account) but very real over a multi-decade horizon. The goal-timeline ladder in this chapter isn't arguing for locking up money you'll need soon; it's arguing against locking up money you don't need soon in an accessible account that's earning less advantage than it could, out of a general, undifferentiated caution that doesn't examine each dollar's actual timeline.

"How do I know if my employer's retirement plan is actually a good deal beyond the match itself?" Look specifically at the plan's available investment options and their fee structure, which vary meaningfully across employers and can materially affect long-run growth even within a tax-advantaged account. This chapter's framework assumes a reasonably low-cost plan; a household with an employer plan carrying unusually high fees beyond the matched portion may have a legitimate case for capturing the match, then directing additional long-horizon savings to a personal tax-advantaged account with lower fees instead of contributing further to the employer plan — a nuance worth discussing with a fee-aware financial professional rather than assuming every employer plan is equally worth maximizing beyond its match.

A note on health savings accounts as a third bucket

Many households have access to a third account type beyond the two this chapter's ladder is built around — a health savings account, available to those enrolled in a qualifying high-deductible health plan, which carries a distinct combination of tax advantages worth folding into this chapter's framework rather than treating as an afterthought. Depending on jurisdiction and specific plan rules, contributions can reduce current taxable income, growth inside the account can be tax-advantaged, and withdrawals for qualified medical expenses can avoid taxation entirely — a combination sometimes referred to informally as triple tax advantage, real and verifiable through current tax-code provisions for these account types, though specific rules and contribution limits should always be checked directly given how often they're adjusted.

Where a household has access to this account type, it's worth treating it, for the specific purpose of long-horizon healthcare-related savings, as at least as favorable as standard retirement accounts, and in some cases more favorable, given the layered tax treatment. A reasonable placement within the goal-timeline ladder from this chapter: after capturing any employer retirement match (Step 1), a health savings account contribution up to any employer-matched portion (if offered) belongs alongside that first-priority tier, given its own strong effective return; contributions beyond any match compete with standard tax-advantaged retirement contributions for the "long-horizon, no near-term goal" allocation described in Step 4, with the specific split between the two account types coming down to each household's confidence in unreimbursed future medical costs versus general retirement income needs — a genuinely individual judgment call, best made with input from a tax professional familiar with your specific plan's rules and your broader financial picture.

A short exercise: mapping your own goals onto the ladder

List every active savings goal you're currently funding or planning to fund, with an honest estimate of its timeline in years. Sort the list from soonest to furthest out. For each goal within roughly five years, default to accessible savings unless there's a specific, well-understood reason to consider a tax-advantaged vehicle with penalty-free early access provisions. For each goal beyond roughly fifteen years, default to tax-advantaged retirement accounts, after confirming any employer match is already fully captured. For anything in between, apply Step 3's test directly: is the timeline firm or flexible, and does that flexibility change how much early-withdrawal risk you're comfortable carrying. This sorted list, revisited whenever a new goal enters the picture or an existing one's timeline shifts, is the practical version of the ladder this chapter describes — not a one-time decision, but a live document that tracks your actual goals as they actually change.

Common objections and how to handle them, continued

"What happens to the accessible-savings portion once its specific goal is fulfilled?" Once a near-term goal is fully funded — the down payment saved, the wedding paid for — the accessible account that had been serving it doesn't need to keep collecting new contributions at the same rate, and the portion of the gap that had been flowing there becomes available for reallocation. Run Step 2 again: is there a new near-term goal to fund, or does the money now belong, per Step 4, in tax-advantaged accounts as long-horizon savings with no specific near-term claim on it? Treating a fulfilled goal's funding stream as a decision point, rather than letting it drift by default into whichever account happens to be easiest to keep contributing to, is the same discipline Chapter 3's account-naming practice applies to any account whose original job has changed.

"Should a starter emergency buffer, distinct from any named goal, count as accessible savings or as its own category in this ladder?" A starter emergency buffer — the kind referenced in Chapter 3's debt-payoff sequencing, and covered in more structural depth in this library's companion volume on automation — functions, for the purposes of this chapter's ladder, as an extremely near-term, always-active "goal" with no fixed date at all, since its entire purpose is being available on short notice. It belongs in accessible savings by definition, ranked ahead of any other near-term goal in Step 2's sort, because its job (absorbing an unplanned shock without derailing everything else) is the one job in this entire framework that can't tolerate an early-withdrawal penalty or a multi-day transfer delay under any circumstance.

"What if I have access to more than one tax-advantaged account type and need to choose between them, not just decide how much goes to tax-advantaged accounts overall?" This chapter's ladder answers the *how much* question — the split between tax-advantaged and accessible — but deliberately doesn't adjudicate between multiple tax-advantaged account types available to the same household (an employer plan versus a personal account, a traditional versus a Roth-style structure), since that choice depends heavily on current versus expected future tax rates, account-specific rules, and individual circumstances that a general mechanics book can't responsibly generalize. Once this chapter's ladder has told you how much belongs in the tax-advantaged bucket overall, a tax professional or a fee-only financial advisor is the right resource for splitting that bucket further across specific account types available to your situation.

A note on limited early-access provisions within retirement accounts

This chapter's ladder treats tax-advantaged retirement accounts as functionally inaccessible before a specified age, and for the purposes of Step 2's near-versus-long-horizon sort, that's the correct conservative assumption to build a plan around. It's worth noting, without contradicting that conservative default, that certain retirement account structures do carry limited, specific early-access provisions beyond a full early-withdrawal penalty — a contribution basis that can sometimes be withdrawn without penalty under specific account types, a defined hardship-withdrawal provision for certain qualifying expenses, or a structured early-distribution method under specific IRS-defined rules for those willing to commit to a fixed, multi-year distribution schedule.

None of these provisions should be treated as making a retirement account a substitute for genuine accessible savings in this chapter's ladder — each carries real restrictions, often significant complexity, and in most cases still forfeits the tax-advantaged growth that was the entire point of using the account in the first place. They're worth knowing about specifically for the middle-distance goal case from Step 3, where a household weighing whether a flexible goal can lean further toward tax-advantaged accounts might reasonably factor in that a true emergency, even one arriving before standard retirement age, isn't necessarily a complete dead end if it ever came to that — a modest additional layer of confidence, not a reason to under-fund genuine accessible savings for any goal that's actually likely to need funding on a firm, foreseeable timeline. Confirm the specific provisions and their real restrictions with a tax professional before treating any of them as part of an active plan.

A worked example: splitting a rate across three simultaneous goals

To show the ladder handling more than two goals at once, consider a household with a $9,200 monthly take-home, a floor of $5,700, and a gap of $3,500 — comfortably in Bracket 3, with a bracket-based rate of roughly $1,610 a month before any goal-specific allocation decisions are made. This household has three simultaneous claims on that rate: standard retirement (30-plus years out), a wedding they're funding for a family member in 18 months (firm date, firm cost of $22,000, already $6,000 saved), and a flexible goal of upgrading their home within the next six to nine years (soft timeline, rough estimate of $40,000).

Applying the ladder in order: Step 1 captures the employer match first, say $480 a month. Step 2 sorts the remaining goals by timeline — the wedding is the clear near-term case, the home upgrade the clear middle-distance case, and standard retirement the clear long-horizon case. Working backward from the wedding's $16,000 remaining need over 18 months requires $889 a month into accessible savings, funded first given its firm, soonest deadline. That leaves $241 of the $1,610 base rate (after the match and the wedding allocation) for the remaining two goals. Applying Step 3's flexible-timeline logic to the home upgrade, given its soft six-to-nine-year window, the household leans this remaining amount roughly 60/40 toward tax-advantaged retirement and accessible home-upgrade savings — $145 and $96 respectively — accepting that the home upgrade will accumulate slowly for now and can be revisited once the wedding is fully funded and that portion of the rate becomes available for reallocation, per Chapter 7's guidance on a fulfilled near-term goal freeing up its funding stream.

This three-goal example makes a point worth stating plainly: the ladder doesn't require picking a single winner among competing goals. It requires ranking them honestly by timeline, funding the firmest and soonest first, and treating whatever remains as a genuine, if sometimes small, allocation to the rest — rather than either ignoring the less urgent goals entirely until the urgent one clears, or splitting evenly across all three in a way that risks under-funding the one with an actual deadline attached.

Chapter 8 — The Diminishing-Returns Ceiling

The situation

A household saving 45% of their income, well above any flat benchmark and comfortably justified by the bracket math in Chapter 2 given their large gap above their fixed-cost floor, has never actually calculated whether 45% is accomplishing anything additional beyond a lower rate. They assume more is simply better, the same unexamined instinct that drives most aggressive savers, and they haven't run the numbers to check whether their current trajectory already clears a realistic retirement target with room to spare — which would mean the marginal dollar going to savings right now is buying very little additional security, at a real, ongoing cost in present quality of life.

The mechanics

This book has spent seven chapters establishing why more saving is usually the correct answer relative to a flat, often-too-low benchmark. It's worth being equally rigorous about the opposite claim: past a genuine, calculable point, additional saving stops producing meaningfully more retirement security and starts trading present well-being for a margin of safety that's already been comfortably achieved. This isn't a claim that anyone can save "too much" in some vague, moralizing sense — it's a specific, calculable statement about the point at which a savings trajectory has already cleared a realistic target, such that continuing to save at the same aggressive rate is a deliberate choice about *how much margin above the target* to hold, not a necessary step toward reaching the target at all.

Establishing where this ceiling sits requires a real target to measure against, not a vague sense of "enough." Retirement-income research consistently points to a replacement-ratio framework: the percentage of pre-retirement income a household needs in retirement to maintain a comparable standard of living, accounting for the fact that several major pre-retirement costs (mortgage principal if paid off by then, retirement-account contributions themselves, certain work-related expenses, payroll taxes on income no longer being earned) typically disappear or shrink substantially. Widely cited research in this area — including work associated with the Georgia State University Retirement Research Center and consistent with broader industry replacement-ratio studies — points to a typical target somewhere in the range of 70 to 85% of pre-retirement income, varying by actual income level and lifestyle, as sufficient to maintain a comparable standard of living into retirement, rather than the intuitively assumed but generally unnecessary 100%.

The framework: calculating and checking against your ceiling

Step 1 — Establish your retirement-income target using a realistic replacement ratio, not an assumed 100% of current income. Apply a replacement ratio in the 70 to 85% range to your current pre-retirement income, adjusted for your specific circumstances — a household with unusually high fixed medical or housing costs projected into retirement may reasonably target the higher end or above it; a household expecting a mortgage to be fully paid off and modest fixed costs may reasonably target the lower end.

Step 2 — Project your current savings trajectory forward to your planned retirement age, using a conservative assumed return, and compare the projected total against the income target from Step 1 converted into a required portfolio size (commonly estimated using a sustainable withdrawal-rate framework — research associated with financial planner William Bengen and later refined by the Trinity Study researchers commonly cites a rate in the general range of 4% annually as a historically sustainable starting withdrawal rate, though this figure carries real debate and should be treated as a planning reference point rather than a guarantee).

Step 3 — If your projected trajectory already clears your target with a reasonable margin, treat any savings rate beyond what's needed to sustain that trajectory as a deliberate choice, not an obligation. This is the actual ceiling this chapter is naming: not a hard number that applies universally, but the specific, calculable point at which your own trajectory has already answered the question "will I have enough," such that additional saving is now purchasing extra margin, an earlier retirement date, or a more generous target — all legitimate things to want, but worth choosing on purpose rather than defaulting into via an unexamined, maximally aggressive rate.

Step 4 — If choosing to continue at a rate beyond the calculated requirement, be explicit about what the excess is actually buying. A household that runs this math and decides to keep saving at 45% anyway, having confirmed their target is already covered by something closer to 30%, isn't making a mistake — they may be deliberately buying an earlier retirement, a larger cushion against uncertain future healthcare costs, or the ability to help fund a goal for another family member. The mistake this chapter is actually warning against isn't a high rate chosen deliberately for a real reason — it's a high rate maintained by default, with real present-day cost, toward a target that was never actually calculated and checked.

Worked example

The household from this chapter's opening earns $11,400 a month take-home, saving 45% ($5,130 a month) toward retirement, with 22 years until their planned retirement age and $310,000 already accumulated. Using a 7% assumed return, their current trajectory projects to roughly $3.4 million by retirement.

Their target, using an 80% replacement ratio against current pre-retirement income (adjusted upward for expected future income growth, then converted to a required portfolio using a 4% sustainable withdrawal reference rate) comes out to approximately $2.6 million. Their projected trajectory of $3.4 million clears this target by roughly $800,000 — a real, meaningful margin, not a marginal or uncertain one.

Running the reverse calculation — what monthly contribution would be required to reach exactly the $2.6 million target rather than the $3.4 million their current rate produces — comes out to roughly $3,400 a month, not $5,130. The household is currently directing an additional $1,730 a month, or roughly $20,760 a year, toward margin beyond their calculated target. That's not automatically wrong — but it's a choice worth making deliberately. If the household genuinely wants the extra margin (a hedge against uncertain healthcare costs, a desire to retire a few years earlier than currently planned, a wish to leave a meaningful inheritance), continuing at 45% is a well-informed decision. If the excess is simply inertia — a rate set years ago and never revisited once the trajectory had already cleared the target — redirecting some of that $1,730 toward present quality of life, a more generous discretionary budget, or a different goal entirely (a home renovation, more travel, more room in a household budget for genuinely valued present-day spending) is equally legitimate, and arguably the more deliberate choice of the two.

A second worked example: recalculating after a ceiling is crossed

A different household discovers, running this chapter's math for the first time, that their current 38% savings rate already produces a projected trajectory nearly 40% above their calculated target — a considerably larger excess than the first example, reflecting a household that has been saving aggressively for over a decade without ever checking the math against an actual target. Rather than treating this as license to abandon saving discipline entirely, they use Step 4 explicitly:

they decide to redirect a portion of the excess — dropping their rate from 38% to 26%, still comfortably above their calculated requirement with a reasonable margin built in — and redirect the freed-up difference toward a mix of increased present discretionary spending and a new medium-term goal (funding a portion of a child's education) that had previously been treated as unaffordable while the household defaulted to maximizing retirement contributions without ever checking whether that maximization was still necessary.

Common objections and how to handle them

"Isn't it safer to just keep saving as much as possible, regardless of what the target calculation says?" "As much as possible" isn't actually free of cost — it's a continuous tradeoff against present quality of life, and treating it as costless simply because the cost doesn't show up as a line item the way an unpaid bill would is a real blind spot, not a form of prudence. This chapter isn't arguing against a healthy margin above a calculated target; it's arguing that the size of that margin should be a deliberate choice, informed by an actual calculation, rather than an assumption that more is definitionally better with no consideration of what's being given up in exchange.

"What if my assumptions about returns or my target turn out to be wrong?" This is a legitimate concern, and it's exactly why Step 3 calls for "a reasonable margin," not a razor-thin one — a household whose projected trajectory clears their target by only a few percentage points hasn't really cleared a meaningful ceiling yet, and should treat their current rate as appropriately calibrated rather than searching for room to reduce it. The ceiling this chapter describes only becomes relevant once the margin is genuinely substantial, not marginal, which is a real and important distinction the worked examples above are built to illustrate.

"Doesn't this chapter contradict the rest of the book, which argues for saving more than a flat rule suggests?" No — it completes the same argument from the other direction. The first seven chapters argue that a flat percentage under-serves households with real room above their floor, who should often be saving considerably more than a flat rule suggests. This chapter argues that even a well-calculated, floor-based rate should eventually be checked against a real target, because "more room to save" and "should keep saving at the maximum sustainable rate indefinitely" are two different claims, and conflating them is its own kind of error — just one that shows up much later, and much more quietly, than under-saving does.

A note on aggressive early-retirement planning and the ceiling

A specific community of savers deliberately targets a savings rate far above anything this chapter's typical worked examples describe — sometimes 50% or more of income — with the explicit goal of reaching financial independence and retiring meaningfully earlier than a standard retirement age. It's worth being precise about how this chapter's ceiling framework relates to that approach, because the two aren't in conflict, even though they can look that way at first glance.

The ceiling described in this chapter is calculated against a specific retirement age and a specific income-replacement target. A household deliberately pursuing an early-retirement date has, in effect, chosen a much shorter timeline and, frequently, a leaner target than a standard retirement plan assumes — which mechanically requires a much higher savings rate to reach, for exactly the same reason Chapter 5's catch-up math shows a compressed timeline requiring a higher monthly contribution. An aggressive rate aimed explicitly at an early, specific target isn't a violation of this chapter's ceiling logic — it's Step 4 in action: a household that has run the numbers, identified precisely what the higher rate is buying (years of freedom from full-time work, not just an arbitrary abstract goal), and chosen it deliberately. The distinction this chapter draws isn't between "high rate" and "low rate" in the abstract — it's between a rate chosen deliberately against a calculated target, whatever that target happens to be, and a rate maintained by inertia long after the calculation that would justify it was ever actually run.

A short exercise: checking your own ceiling

Using your current savings rate, current balance, and years until your planned retirement age, project your trajectory forward using a conservative assumed return. Separately, calculate a target using a 70-to-85% replacement ratio against your current income and a sustainable withdrawal-rate conversion, per this chapter's method. Compare the two. If your projected trajectory falls short of the target, your current rate is appropriately calibrated or possibly still too low — return to Chapter 2's bracket math and Chapter 5's catch-up framework rather than this chapter's ceiling logic. If your projected trajectory clears the target by a substantial, comfortable margin, decide explicitly, using Step 4's framework, whether the excess is buying something you actually want — an earlier retirement, a larger cushion, a legacy goal — or whether it's simply an old rate that's never been checked against a real number until now.

A note on non-financial ceilings this chapter doesn't calculate

Everything in this chapter's framework calculates a ceiling against a single kind of target — a retirement-income replacement ratio, converted into a required portfolio size. It's worth being explicit that this is a genuinely narrower question than "how much should I save overall," because a full financial picture includes goals a replacement-ratio calculation doesn't touch at all: funding a portion of a child's education, leaving a deliberate inheritance, building a cushion against an anticipated future caregiving responsibility, or simply valuing the psychological security of a larger buffer than the bare retirement math requires. None of these are irrational or undisciplined reasons to save beyond the calculated retirement ceiling — they're separate, legitimate targets that deserve their own explicit calculation rather than being folded silently into "more retirement savings just in case."

The practical fix, consistent with this book's broader method, is the same one applied throughout: name the goal specifically, estimate its cost and timeline the way Chapter 7's goal-timeline ladder does for any other goal, and fund it as its own deliberate line item rather than letting an unexamined "keep the retirement rate high, just in case" serve as a stand-in for a goal that was never actually specified. A household that wants to leave $200,000 to their children has a genuinely different, calculable target than a household maximizing retirement security alone, and the two targets, added together explicitly, produce a combined ceiling that's meaningfully more honest than either an unexamined high rate or a narrowly calculated retirement-only ceiling on its own.

A second worked example: two households at the same ceiling, different choices

Two households, each with a projected trajectory clearing their calculated retirement target by roughly the same 30% margin, make different, equally legitimate choices once they've run this chapter's ceiling check. The first decides the margin is exactly the cushion they want against uncertain future healthcare costs and continues their current rate unchanged, having now confirmed explicitly what the excess is for rather than continuing on inertia alone. The second decides the margin is larger than they need for any specific goal they can name, and redirects roughly half of the excess toward a mix of increased present-day discretionary spending and a new medium-term goal — a long-deferred home renovation — funded through Chapter 7's goal-timeline ladder as its own explicit line item. Both households ran the identical calculation and arrived at the identical ceiling. What differed was the deliberate choice made once the number was in hand — which is precisely the outcome this chapter is built to produce: not a single correct answer for what to do with a margin above target, but an informed, explicit decision instead of an unexamined default in either direction.

A note on market downturns and how much margin actually protects against them

A fair question to raise against this entire chapter: doesn't a real market downturn, arriving at an inconvenient time, erode exactly the kind of comfortable margin this chapter is describing, making the whole ceiling calculation fragile rather than solid. This deserves a direct answer rather than being waved away, because it's precisely the right kind of skepticism to bring to a projection built on an assumed average return that real markets never actually deliver in a smooth, uninterrupted line.

The honest answer is that a margin calculated using this chapter's method is, among other things, exactly the kind of cushion that absorbs a real downturn without requiring a change in retirement plans. A household whose trajectory clears their target by 30% has real room to absorb a market decline of considerably less than 30% in the years immediately before or after retirement without falling below the actual target itself — which is a different and more resilient position than a household whose trajectory lands exactly at the target with no margin at all, where the identical downturn pushes the actual outcome below the real need. This is, in fact, one of the legitimate, specific reasons a household might choose, in Step 4's deliberate-choice framework, to hold a margin rather than redirect all of it elsewhere: not vague caution, but a specific, nameable purpose — sequence-of-returns risk in the years around retirement, when a downturn does the most damage to a portfolio that's also being drawn down for income. Naming this specific risk explicitly, and deciding how much margin it justifies holding, is a more honest approach than either ignoring downturn risk entirely or treating it as a reason to abandon this chapter's ceiling logic altogether.

A note on recalculating the ceiling after retirement actually begins

Everything in this chapter is framed as a pre-retirement calculation — projecting a trajectory forward, comparing it against a target, deciding what to do with any margin while still actively saving. It's worth closing with a brief note on what happens to this same logic once retirement actually arrives, since the ceiling question doesn't simply disappear the day regular contributions stop; it shifts into a related but distinct question about withdrawal rather than accumulation.

Once retirement begins, the sustainable withdrawal-rate research referenced throughout this chapter — the same body of work underlying the 4% planning reference point — becomes the primary tool rather than the accumulation-side projection this chapter has focused on. A retiree whose portfolio sits meaningfully above their calculated target at the start of retirement is, in effect, carrying the same kind of margin this chapter describes into the withdrawal phase, and that margin functions similarly: room to weather a downturn in the early retirement years without needing to cut spending, room to increase withdrawals modestly if the portfolio performs well, or room to leave a larger legacy than originally planned if the margin is never actually needed. The specific mechanics of managing a withdrawal rate through retirement — adjusting for market performance year to year, sequencing withdrawals across different account types — are genuinely their own subject, beyond what this book's savings-rate focus is built to cover in full; the point worth carrying forward from this chapter is simply that the ceiling calculation doesn't end the day contributions stop. It transforms into a related question about how much of that calculated cushion to actually spend, and that question deserves the same explicit, deliberate treatment this chapter has argued for throughout the accumulation years.

Chapter 9 — The Decision Framework: Run Your Own Numbers

The situation

Every chapter in this book has covered one piece of the calculation — the floor test, the bracket math, the debt overlay, the transition reset, the catch-up multiplier, the trailing average for variable income, the retirement-versus-accessible split, and the ceiling check. This final chapter threads all of it into a single, ordered sequence, so a reader with a real, specific situation can run through it start to finish and arrive at an actual number, rather than holding eight separate frameworks in their head and guessing at how they combine.

The mechanics

The reason this book builds toward a single sequence rather than presenting eight independent tools is that real situations rarely involve just one of these mechanics in isolation. A household might be carrying debt, mid-transition, and uncertain whether they're above or below their eventual ceiling, all at the same time. Running each chapter's framework separately, without a clear order, risks double-counting some adjustments and missing others entirely. This chapter fixes the order.

The framework: the full sequence

Step 1 — Calculate your true fixed-cost floor (Chapter 1). Pull real statements, separate genuine floor costs from discretionary ones, and arrive at an honest number — not aspirational, not punitive.

Step 2 — If you're mid-transition (Chapter 4), recalculate the floor specifically for your current, transitional reality, not your prior or anticipated future baseline. Use the transition-specific floor for every subsequent step until your review date arrives.

Step 3 — If your income is variable (Chapter 6), calculate your trailing twelve-month post-tax average and use that, not your most recent single month, as the income figure for every subsequent step.

Step 4 — Calculate your gap: income (from Step 3 if applicable) minus floor (from Step 2 if applicable).

Step 5 — Identify your bracket and baseline sustainable rate as a percentage of the gap (Chapter 2).

Step 6 — If you're carrying debt above the roughly 7-to-9% investment-return threshold (Chapter 3), reallocate the majority of your gap toward that debt first, after capturing any employer match, until it's cleared — then return to Step 5's bracket math using your post-debt gap.

Step 7 — If you're starting later than a standard timeline assumes (Chapter 5), run the catch-up calculation against your actual target and years remaining, and compare it to the rate produced by Step 5 or Step 6 — adjust using the three levers (timeline, target, contribution) if the gap between them is large.

Step 8 — Split your resulting rate between tax-advantaged retirement accounts and accessible savings using the goal-timeline ladder (Chapter 7), capturing any employer match first regardless of anything else in the sequence.

Step 9 — Check your resulting trajectory against a realistic retirement-income target using a replacement-ratio calculation (Chapter 8). If your trajectory clears the target with a substantial margin, treat any rate beyond what the target requires as a deliberate choice, and decide explicitly whether to maintain it, redirect part of it, or hold it as intentional extra margin.

Step 10 — Set a review date. Any transition-specific adjustment from Step 2 needs a calendared reassessment. Beyond that, a full rerun of this entire sequence at least annually, or any time income, fixed costs, debt, or goals shift meaningfully, keeps the resulting rate accurate rather than stale.

Worked example: the full sequence, start to finish

A worker earns a trailing twelve-month post-tax average income (Step 3 applies, since a portion of the year included freelance side income alongside a primary salary) of $6,900 a month. Their fixed-cost floor (Step 1), unaffected by any current transition, is $4,300. Their gap (Step 4) is $2,600.

They're carrying $9,000 in credit-card debt at 21% APR (Step 6 applies). After capturing their full employer match (a fixed $310 a month off the top), they direct 80% of the remaining $2,600 gap — $2,072 — toward the credit card, clearing it in roughly five months given the balance and rate. During those five months, general savings continue at a minimal level using the remaining 20% of the post-match gap, roughly $518 a month.

Once the debt clears in month five, the floor drops (the minimum payment folded into it disappears), widening the gap to roughly $2,950. Recalculating the bracket (Step 5) against this new, larger gap places the household solidly in Bracket 3, with a sustainable rate around 46% of the gap: roughly $1,357 a month, on top of the $310 already captured for the employer match — a combined $1,667 a month moving forward.

They're 38 years old, planning to retire at 65 (Step 7 applies as a sanity check, though not as an urgent catch-up case at this age) — running the standard compound calculation against their target confirms their new rate, sustained consistently, comfortably reaches a reasonable target well before the deadline, so no adjustment to the three levers is needed at this stage.

Applying the goal-timeline ladder (Step 8): beyond the captured employer match, they have one middle-distance goal (a possible home purchase, roughly eight years out, with a flexible rather than firm timeline) and no other near-term goals. Given the flexible timeline, they split the remaining $1,357 roughly 55/45 toward tax-advantaged retirement and accessible savings for the home goal — $746 and $611 respectively.

Checking against the ceiling (Step 9): their full projected trajectory, combining existing savings, the employer match, and this new rate, is run against an 80% replacement-ratio target for their current income level. The projection clears the target by a modest, not dramatic, margin — meaningful enough to feel reasonably confident, but not so large that Chapter 8's ceiling logic calls for redirecting funds elsewhere. No adjustment is made; the current rate stands as calculated.

A review date (Step 10) is set for twelve months out, with an earlier check built in at month five when the debt payoff is expected to complete and the gap recalculation from that milestone needs to actually happen rather than being assumed.

Running the sequence when nothing complicated applies

Not every reader's situation involves debt above the threshold, an active transition, a late start, or variable income — and it's worth showing the sequence for the simplest realistic case, since the ten steps can look more intimidating in the abstract than they turn out to be in practice when several of them simply don't apply.

A worker earns a stable $5,600 a month take-home (Step 3 doesn't apply — income is stable, not variable), with a fixed-cost floor of $3,700 (Step 1, no transition adjustment needed, so Step 2 is skipped), for a gap of $1,900 (Step 4). No debt above the investment-return threshold exists (Step 6 is skipped entirely), so the bracket calculation from Step 5 applies directly: a gap that's 34% of income places this worker just under the Bracket 3 threshold, in upper Bracket 2, with a sustainable rate around 34% of the gap — $646 a month. At 29 years old with a standard retirement age of 65, the catch-up check in Step 7 confirms this rate comfortably reaches a reasonable target well ahead of schedule, so no adjustment is needed there either.

Applying the goal-timeline ladder in Step 8: the worker captures their full employer match first (a fixed $180 a month), with the remaining $466 split toward long-horizon retirement, since there's no active near- or middle-distance goal currently competing for accessible savings. The ceiling check in Step 9 shows the resulting trajectory clearing a realistic replacement-ratio target without a dramatic excess margin, so the full calculated rate stands as-is. A review date (Step 10) is set for twelve months out, with no earlier interim checkpoint needed since nothing about the current situation is in flux.

Five of the ten steps did real work in this case — the floor and gap calculation, the bracket placement, the catch-up sanity check, the goal-timeline split, and the ceiling check. The other five simply confirmed they didn't apply and moved on. This is the normal shape of running the sequence for most straightforward situations: not every step requires a calculation every time, but running through the full list, even briefly, catches the cases where something that looked irrelevant at first glance — a debt that's actually above the threshold, a transition that's closer than it seemed — turns out to matter after all.

A short exercise: your own full sequence

Work through all ten steps in this chapter against your own real numbers, in order, writing down the result of each step even when a step doesn't apply to your situation (write "not applicable" rather than skipping it silently — this matters, because it forces a deliberate check rather than an assumption). By the end, you'll have a single monthly savings rate, split across whatever accounts your goal-timeline ladder calls for, along with an explicit review date. Compare the resulting number to whatever flat percentage you'd absorbed before picking up this book. The difference between the two — whether your calculated rate turns out higher, lower, or close to what you'd been told to aim for — is the actual, concrete value this book was built to hand you: not a replacement rule to follow blindly instead of the old one, but a method that produces the number that's actually correct for the situation you're really in.

What this sequence replaces

It's worth being explicit, at the close of this book, about what this ten-step sequence is actually standing in for. It replaces a single borrowed number — 20%, or 15%, or whatever specific figure happened to reach a given reader first — with a calculation built entirely from that reader's own real numbers: their actual floor, their actual debt, their actual life stage, their actual income pattern, their actual goals, and their actual target. No two households running this sequence with different inputs will land on the same output, and that's not a flaw in the method. It's the entire point. A single flat rule was never going to be right for every income, every debt load, every life stage, and every goal at once, because no single number can be. This sequence doesn't promise a universally correct answer. It promises a correctly calculated one, for the specific situation it's run against — which is the only kind of answer a savings rate was ever going to be able to honestly give.

A closing note on revisiting this sequence

This chapter's ten steps aren't meant to be run once and filed away. Every input changes over a working life — income rises and sometimes falls, debt gets taken on and paid off, transitions arrive and resolve, goals shift as circumstances shift. The sequence itself doesn't change; what changes, every time you run it again, are the numbers you feed into it. That's a feature of a genuinely mechanical framework, not a flaw: the same ten steps that produced the right rate for a 28-year-old with no debt and a stable salary will produce an entirely different, equally correct rate for the same person at 45, with a mortgage, two kids, and a decade of catch-up math to run. Rerun it. The math will tell you what's changed.

Common objections and how to handle them

"Ten steps feels like a lot to run through every time something changes." Most of the ten steps, as the simple worked example above showed, resolve in a sentence or two once you've confirmed they don't apply to your current situation — the sequence only takes real time to work through when several steps genuinely do apply at once, which is exactly the situation where a flat percentage would have failed you most badly anyway. A full rerun, done carefully the first time and then updated incrementally as specific inputs change, typically takes less time than a single hour once the initial floor and gap calculations from Chapter 1 are already on file and just need updating rather than rebuilding from scratch.

"What if I disagree with one of the specific percentages or thresholds used in this book's frameworks — the 7-to-9% debt threshold, the bracket ranges, the 70-to-85% replacement ratio?" Every specific figure in this book's frameworks is a reasonable, research-grounded starting point, not an immovable constant, and the sequence in this chapter works identically with a reader's own preferred figures substituted in. A reader with a more conservative view of long-run investment returns can lower the debt threshold in Step 6 accordingly; a reader with a specific, well-researched view of their own retirement-income needs can substitute a different replacement ratio in Step 9. The mechanics — the order of operations, the logic connecting a floor to a gap to a bracket to a rate — are what this book is actually built to teach. The specific numbers plugged into that structure should always be the reader's own best, current information, updated as better information becomes available.

"How is this sequence different from just hiring a financial planner to tell me a number?" A good financial planner is doing a version of this same calculation, informed by training and experience this book can't fully replace, particularly for genuinely complex situations — multiple income sources, significant assets, complicated tax situations, or major estate considerations. What this chapter's sequence offers that a single planner conversation often doesn't is a repeatable method you can rerun yourself, for free, every time a real input changes, without needing to schedule a new appointment for every incremental update. The two aren't mutually exclusive: a reader with access to a qualified financial planner can bring this chapter's calculated rate into that conversation as a well-informed starting point, which tends to produce a more productive conversation than arriving with no number in hand at all, or with only a borrowed flat percentage to compare against.

"What if two of the chapters this sequence draws on seem to give conflicting guidance for my specific situation?" This shouldn't happen if the ten-step order is followed as written, since the sequence itself was built specifically to resolve the handful of real interactions between chapters — Chapter 5's note on running catch-up math alongside Chapter 3's debt-payoff priority is one explicit example, worked out in full in that chapter rather than left for the reader to guess at. If you find a genuine conflict this book's sequence doesn't already address, the general resolution principle used throughout is this: a guaranteed, near-term mechanical benefit (an employer match, clearing genuinely high-interest debt) generally outranks an uncertain, longer-horizon one, and a firm, dated obligation generally outranks a flexible, aspirational one. Applying that same ordering logic to a situation this book hasn't explicitly worked through will, in almost every case, produce the same answer this book's own sequence would have.

A note on using this sequence with a partner or household, not just as an individual

Every worked example in this chapter is written from the perspective of a single decision-maker running the sequence against a single set of numbers, but many readers are making these decisions jointly with a partner, and it's worth being explicit about how the sequence adapts. The floor-and-gap calculation in Step 1 should already reflect the full household, as Chapter 2's second worked example on two-income households demonstrated — combined income against a combined floor, not two separate parallel calculations that then need to be reconciled. Steps 6 through 9, however, often involve decisions specific to one partner's accounts, employer benefits, or individual goals, and those steps may need to be run once per partner even while Steps 1 through 5 are run jointly for the household as a whole. A practical approach: run Steps 1 through 5 together, as a single household calculation, then split into individual tracks for Steps 6 through 8 wherever employer-specific benefits or individually held debt are involved, and reconverge for Step 9's ceiling check, run against the household's combined trajectory and combined target rather than two separate individual ones. The sequence doesn't need to be rebuilt from scratch for a household of two — it needs one deliberate decision about which steps are joint and which are individual, made once and then reused every time the sequence gets rerun.

A final worked walkthrough: revisiting a plan five years later

To close the loop on this chapter's central claim — that the sequence, not any single output, is the lasting tool — it's worth showing the same household from this chapter's first full worked example five years later, running the sequence again rather than assuming the original numbers still hold. Their trailing-average income has grown to $8,900 a month as their consulting practice has matured (Step 3 still applies). Their floor, after a modest move to a slightly larger home, is now $5,600 (Step 1, no active transition — Step 2 skipped). Their gap is $3,300, comfortably in Bracket 3.

The high-interest debt from the original example cleared years ago and never returned, so Step 6 is skipped entirely this time. At 43, with retirement still planned for 65, Step 7's catch-up check confirms their current trajectory remains on track without requiring lever adjustments. The home goal from Step 8's original calculation was fulfilled three years ago; that portion of the gap has since been redirected, per Chapter 7's guidance on a fulfilled goal, into additional tax-advantaged retirement contributions, alongside a new middle-distance goal — funding part of a child's future education, roughly nine years out — split according to Step 3's flexible-versus-firm timeline test. Step 9's ceiling check shows their trajectory clearing their retirement target by a modest, reasonable margin, not a dramatic one, so the full calculated rate stands without adjustment. A new review date is set, and the cycle continues.

Nothing about the ten-step sequence itself changed across those five years. Every single input did. That's the entire argument this book has been making since its opening chapter, run one more time, with real numbers, to show it holds up over an actual stretch of a real financial life — not just in a single, isolated calculation, but as a method built to be returned to, again and again, for as long as the numbers keep changing, which they will, for as long as you're earning, saving, and planning for anything at all.

A note on keeping a simple written record across reruns

One practical habit worth adopting alongside this chapter's sequence: keep a brief, dated written record each time you run it — the resulting floor, gap, bracket, rate, and split, along with a one-line note on which steps applied and which didn't. This doesn't need to be elaborate; a single page, updated at each review, is enough. Its value shows up specifically at the next rerun, when having last year's numbers on hand alongside this year's makes it immediately obvious how much has actually changed and why, rather than requiring the floor-and-gap calculation to be rebuilt entirely from memory or from scratch each time.

This same written record also becomes useful in exactly the moment described at the start of this chapter's closing worked example — a real conversation with a financial planner, a partner, or simply your own future self trying to remember why a rate was set where it was. A rate justified by a specific, dated calculation is easy to trust and easy to revisit; a rate that's simply "what it's always been" invites exactly the kind of unexamined inertia Chapter 8's ceiling logic warns against. The record doesn't need to be sophisticated. It needs to exist, and it needs to be updated honestly every time the sequence runs, which is the same discipline this entire book has been built to instill from its opening chapter forward.

Before You Close This Book

Nine chapters, one underlying argument running through all of them: a savings rate isn't a number you inherit from a podcast, a parent, or a headline. It's a calculation, built from your actual fixed costs, your actual debt, your actual life stage, your actual income pattern, and your actual goals — and it's a calculation that changes, correctly, every time any of those inputs change.

This isn't a comfortable conclusion for anyone hoping this book would simply hand over a single better number to replace the flawed one everyone's heard a thousand times. It won't, because that number doesn't exist — not because the math is unknowable, but because the correct answer genuinely differs from household to household in ways a flat percentage was never built to capture. What this book hands over instead is the method for calculating your own, correctly, and the confidence to defend that number against a flat rule that was never actually built with your situation in mind.

It's worth being honest about what doesn't change once you've run the math in this book. The discomfort of watching a strong month's income get partly redirected instead of fully spent doesn't disappear just because the rate behind it is well-calculated. The frustration of a late start doesn't vanish just because Chapter 5 shows you the exact levers available to close the gap. What changes is that the number in front of you is finally an honest one — built from your real floor, your real debt, your real timeline — instead of a borrowed one that was quietly asking too much of you, or quietly asking too little, the entire time.

There's a broader habit worth carrying out of this book, past the specific numbers in any single chapter. Every financial rule that arrives as a single, universal figure — save this percentage, spend this much on housing, retire with this multiple of your salary — deserves the same treatment this book gave to "save 20%": not automatic rejection, and not automatic compliance, but the question of what denominator the rule is actually calculated against, and whether that denominator matches your real situation. Some flat rules will hold up reasonably well under that scrutiny. Many won't, for exactly the reason this book's opening chapter demonstrated: a rule built for an average household's average expenses is, definitionally, wrong for almost every actual household, because almost no household is exactly average. The habit of checking a borrowed number against your own real math, rather than accepting or rejecting it on faith, is the actual product this book is handing you — more durable than any single percentage, and useful for far more than just this specific question.

There's one more thing worth saying plainly before you close this book, because it's easy to lose sight of amid nine chapters of arithmetic: the point of getting this number right was never the number itself. It was always what the number lets you stop worrying about. A correctly calculated rate, sustained because it's actually sustainable rather than aspirational, means the question "am I saving enough" stops being a source of recurring, low-grade anxiety and becomes something you can answer, plainly and specifically, any time it comes up — because you've already done the math, and the math is real. That's worth more than the specific dollar figure sitting in any single account, and it's the actual reason this book spent nine chapters building a method instead of just handing over a better guess.

Run the sequence in Chapter 9 with your real numbers. Not the numbers you wish you had, and not the numbers a flat rule assumes you have — the real ones, pulled from your own statements and your own situation. Then run it again next year, and the year after that, as those real numbers change. That's the whole method. It was never going to be one number for everyone, and now you have a way to calculate your own.

Notes & Further Reading

This book draws on established, verifiable research in behavioral finance, retirement planning, and personal-finance practitioner frameworks throughout. Readers interested in going deeper are pointed to the original sources rather than secondary summaries.

On age-based and milestone-based savings benchmarks: Fidelity Investments publishes widely cited, regularly updated age-based savings milestones (commonly summarized as target multiples of annual salary saved by specific ages, working toward roughly ten times annual salary by age 67), used throughout the financial-planning industry as a comparison benchmark. T. Rowe Price publishes a comparable set of age-based benchmarks through its own retirement research. Both are referenced in this book as examples of benchmark tools worth using as a rough comparison point, per the distinction drawn in Chapter 1 between a benchmark for comparison and a rule to force compliance with regardless of individual circumstances.

On the flat-percentage savings rule and its popular framing: Elizabeth Warren and Amelia Warren Tyagi's *All Your Worth: The Ultimate Lifetime Money Plan* (2005) is the origin of the widely cited 50/30/20 budgeting framework (50% needs, 30% wants, 20% savings and debt repayment), which underlies much of the popular "save 20%" framing this book examines critically in Chapter 1. Dave Ramsey's *The Total Money Makeover* similarly popularizes a specific savings percentage (commonly 15% into retirement accounts within his broader "Baby Steps" framework) as part of a widely followed practitioner system. Ramit Sethi's *I Will Teach You To Be Rich* proposes a comparable but distinct percentage-based framework (a "conscious spending plan" allocating roughly 50 to 60% to fixed costs, 10% to investments, 5 to 10% to savings goals, and the remainder to guilt-free spending). This book references all three as real, influential, widely followed frameworks, and its critique in Chapter 1 is specifically that a single flat percentage — whichever version a reader has absorbed — doesn't account for the fixed-cost floor beneath it, not that these practitioners' broader frameworks lack value.

On retirement-income replacement ratios: Research associated with the Georgia State University Retirement Research Center's ongoing Replacement Ratio Study (RRS), conducted in partnership with Aon, is a widely cited source for retirement-income replacement-ratio research, underlying the target-setting method used in Chapter 8. Employee Benefit Research Institute (EBRI) publications on retirement income adequacy provide additional, independently conducted research in the same area, useful as a cross-check against any single study's specific figures.

On sustainable withdrawal rates in retirement: Financial planner William Bengen's original research on sustainable withdrawal rates, first published in the *Journal of Financial Planning* in 1994, is the origin of what's commonly referred to as the "4% rule," referenced in Chapter 8's discussion of converting a retirement-income target into a required portfolio size. The later Trinity Study, conducted by finance professors Philip Cooley, Carl Hubbard, and Daniel Walz at Trinity University and first published in 1998, further tested and refined this research using historical market data. Readers should note that both bodies of research have been subject to ongoing academic debate and refinement in the decades since original publication, and this book presents the 4% figure as a widely used planning reference point, not a guaranteed outcome.

On compound growth and the mathematics of delayed investing: The compound-interest calculations referenced throughout Chapter 5 follow standard, widely available future-value-of-an-annuity formulas taught in any introductory finance curriculum; readers wanting to run their own precise numbers are pointed to reputable, free retirement calculators published by major financial institutions and to standard compound-interest reference formulas rather than a single proprietary source.

On self-employment and variable-income financial planning: The U.S. Internal Revenue Service publishes official guidance on self-employment tax obligations and quarterly estimated tax requirements, referenced generally in Chapter 6; readers with active self-employment income should consult current IRS guidance directly, along with a qualified tax professional, since specific rates and thresholds are adjusted periodically.

On catch-up contribution provisions for retirement accounts: The IRS publishes official, regularly updated guidance on catch-up contribution eligibility and limits for tax-advantaged retirement accounts, referenced generally in Chapter 5; specific dollar limits and eligibility ages are adjusted periodically and should be verified directly through current IRS guidance or a plan administrator rather than any figure that might otherwise be quoted here and go stale.

On household saving behavior and national savings trends: The U.S. Bureau of Economic Analysis publishes the personal saving rate as part of its regular national income and product accounts data, a useful real-world reference point for how national average savings behavior has moved over time, referenced generally in this book's broader discussion of why flat national averages don't translate cleanly into individual household guidance. Vanguard's annual "How America Saves" report, drawing on aggregated data from its retirement plan recordkeeping business, is a widely cited industry source on actual retirement-account contribution and balance patterns across a large sample of real savers. The Federal Reserve's Survey of Consumer Finances, conducted periodically, provides comprehensive, independently gathered data on household balance sheets, savings, and debt across the income distribution, useful as a broader cross-check on the bracket-based patterns discussed in Chapter 2.

On high-interest debt versus investment return comparisons: The general comparison between guaranteed debt-payoff returns and historical long-run diversified investment returns, discussed in Chapter 3, draws on widely available historical return data for broad market indices over multi-decade periods; readers wanting a specific, current comparison for their own debt's interest rate should consult a fee-only financial planner rather than relying on any single historical average as a guarantee of future results.

On Social Security benefit estimation: The U.S. Social Security Administration provides official, individualized benefit estimates based on a worker's own earnings record through its own publicly available tools, referenced in Chapter 5's discussion of incorporating an expected Social Security benefit into a late-starter's catch-up calculation. Readers should use the Administration's own current tools directly rather than any generic estimate, since an accurate figure depends entirely on an individual's specific earnings history and claiming-age decision.

On health savings accounts and their tax treatment: The tax treatment of health savings accounts referenced in Chapter 7 — the ability for contributions, growth, and qualified withdrawals to each receive favorable tax treatment under current U.S. tax law for those enrolled in a qualifying high-deductible health plan — is governed by official IRS guidance, which should be consulted directly for current eligibility rules and contribution limits, both of which are adjusted periodically.

On employer retirement plan vesting rules: Vesting schedules for employer-matched retirement contributions, referenced in Chapter 5's discussion of catch-up planning around a possible job change, are governed in the United States by rules under the Employee Retirement Income Security Act (ERISA) that set maximum allowable vesting timelines, though specific plans may vest faster than the maximum allowed;

readers should confirm their own plan's specific vesting schedule directly through their plan administrator's official plan documents rather than assuming a standard timeline.

A methodological note on how sources were used in writing this book: every named researcher, institution, book, or study cited above was verified against its actual, publicly documented existence and general findings before being included here. No statistic, percentage, or specific study finding appears anywhere in this book's chapters without a traceable source in this section. Passages describing general mechanics without a specific citation attached — the fixed-cost floor test in Chapter 1, the bracket math in Chapter 2, the goal-timeline ladder in Chapter 7 — reflect the author's own applied framework, built from standard financial arithmetic and practitioner experience, and are presented explicitly as that, not disguised as independently published research findings.

A note on the dollar figures, percentages, and assumed rates of return used throughout the worked examples in every chapter: they are illustrative only, chosen to make each mechanism concrete and easy to follow, not to represent verified current benchmarks, guaranteed returns, or advice to apply directly to your own plan. Actual investment returns vary meaningfully year to year and are never guaranteed at any specific figure, including the 7% planning assumption used in several chapters. Readers should always substitute their own researched numbers and, for anything involving tax treatment, retirement-account rules, or investment selection, consult a qualified, licensed professional rather than treating any example in this book as personalized advice.

This book is not legal, tax, investment, or financial advice, and nothing in it should be treated as a guarantee of any specific retirement outcome or savings result. Tax treatment of retirement accounts, contribution limits, and withdrawal rules vary by jurisdiction, account type, and change over time; readers are strongly encouraged to consult a qualified financial advisor, accountant, or tax professional before making significant decisions based on the frameworks in this book.

About

The Savings Rate Playbook is part of the Wealth Mechanics library — a series covering the concrete, learnable mechanics behind everyday money decisions: negotiation, debt payoff, pricing, automated saving systems, and, in this volume, the specific arithmetic behind how much to actually save. Where some books explore the psychology behind why money decisions feel hard, Wealth Mechanics stays entirely in the math: what to actually calculate, in what order, and why the result is correct for your specific numbers rather than an average household's.

Every book in this library follows the same shape — a real situation, the mechanics underneath it, a concrete framework or formula you can apply immediately, and a worked example showing it applied start to finish with real numbers. None of them ask you to become a different kind of saver, spender, or negotiator before you can use them. They're built to be reopened whenever the specific calculation they cover becomes relevant again — a new job, a new debt, a new life stage, a number that's started to feel wrong without your being able to say exactly why.

Daniel Cross writes the Wealth Mechanics library from the practitioner's side of the spreadsheet — years spent building real savings and debt-payoff plans for people whose income, debt, and goals never quite matched whatever generic benchmark they'd been handed, and an equal number of years watching how much better those plans got once the math was actually built from their own numbers instead of borrowed from somewhere else. The pen name reflects the series' identity rather than a single individual's biography: a direct, arithmetic-first voice focused entirely on usable calculations, distinct in both subject and style from the psychological, pattern-diagnosis approach of this studio's sibling series, The Money Instinct, which explores the wired-in reflexes behind money behavior rather than the specific math behind a given financial decision.

This volume sits closest to its immediate predecessor in the library, *The Automatic Wealth System*, and it's worth being clear about how the two divide the territory. That book answers the mechanical question of how to make saving happen automatically, without relying on willpower — the account architecture, the transfer triggers, the sequencing that turns a decided-upon rate into a system that runs itself. This book answers the question that has to be settled first: what rate should actually get automated, given your real income, real debt, real life stage, and real goals. A reader who already has a number in mind and wants to build the system around it is better served starting with the automation volume. A reader who isn't yet confident the number itself is correct — the more common starting point, and the reason this book exists — is better served starting here, and can move to the automation volume once Chapter 9's decision sequence has produced a rate worth building a system around.

This volume also connects, more loosely, to the debt-payoff mechanics covered in *The Debt Freedom System*, elsewhere in this library. That book covers the full mechanics of ordering and accelerating payoff across multiple debts once the decision to prioritize payoff has been made; Chapter 3 of this book covers a narrower, adjacent question — how much of an available savings gap should be redirected toward payoff in the first place, relative to ordinary saving, given a debt's specific interest rate.

A reader actively working through a multi-debt payoff plan is better served by that dedicated volume for the payoff-ordering mechanics themselves; this book's Chapter 3 is the piece that decides how aggressively to fund that plan out of an otherwise-calculated savings rate, not how to sequence the debts once the funding is decided.

Readers new to the Wealth Mechanics library are welcome to start with any volume that matches their most immediate question rather than reading in numbered order — each book stands fully on its own, with no assumed prior reading, and cross-references a companion volume only where the territory genuinely overlaps, as flagged explicitly above.

Future volumes in the Wealth Mechanics library will apply the same situation-mechanics-framework-example structure to other closed, calculable domains of everyday money decisions that most people only work through a handful of times in a life, or get wrong the first time for lack of a clear method. Each volume stands on its own and requires no prior volume to use.

Also in the Series

Every book in Wealth Mechanics stands on its own — read them in any order. If this one was useful, the library continues:

The Negotiation Playbook

The Debt Freedom System

The Pricing Playbook

The Automatic Wealth System

The Investment Onboarding Playbook

The Side Income Playbook

The Real Estate Entry Playbook

The Tax Reduction Playbook

The Equity Compensation Playbook

www.ingramcontent.com/pod-product-compliance
Lightning Source LLC
LaVergne TN
LVHW010720061126
851857LV00014B/1268
9781804281253